Considering the Horse

Considering the *Horse*

Tales of Problems Solved and Lessons Learned

2nd Edition, Revised and Updated

Mark Rashid
Illustrated by Ron Ball

Skyhorse Publishing

Copyright © 1993, 2010, 2014 by Mark Rashid

Illustrations: Ron Ball

Skyhorse Publishing books may be purchased in bulk at special discounts for sales promotion, corporate gifts, fund-raising, or educational purposes. Special editions can also be created to specifications. For details, contact the Special Sales Department, Skyhorse Publishing, 307 West 36th Street, 11th Floor, New York, NY 10018 or info@skyhorse-publishing.com.

Skyhorse® and Skyhorse Publishing® are registered trademarks of Skyhorse Publishing, Inc.®, a Delaware corporation.

Visit our website at www.skyhorsepublishing.com.

10 9 8 7 6 5 4 3

Paperback ISBN: 978-1-62873-721-9

The Library of Congress has cataloged the hardcover edition as follows:

Rashid, Mark.
    Considering the horse : tales of problems solved and lessons learned / Mark Rashid ; illustrated by Ron Ball.
        p. cm.
    ISBN 978-1-61608-156-0
    1. Horses—Training. 2. Horses—Behavior. 3. Western horses—Training. 4. Western horses—Behavior. I. Title.
    SF287.R27 2010
    636.1/0835
                    2010020913

Printed in China

*To my wife, Wendy, my daughter, Lindsey,
and my sons, Tyler and Aaron. Thank you.*

Table of contents

PART TWO: GROUND PROBLEMS

PART THREE: RIDING PROBLEMS

PART FOUR: THE FINAL PROBLEM

Illustrations

Foreword

I guess I've known Mark Rashid for eight or nine years, during which time we've ridden many a trail together, worked a bunch of horses, raised five weanling foals, picked guitars, sang up a storm, and managed to share a brew or two. I've watched him develop from a good horseman into a top hand when it comes to any kind of problem with a horse.

Mind you now, that I had been cowboying, wrangling dudes, and working horses at various places in the Colorado and Wyoming mountains for more than six years when Mark was born! I consider myself to be a fair hand around a horse, but I don't hold a candle to Mark, and it seems the most natural thing in the world for me to consult with him if I have a horse-related problem of any kind.

When Mark first told me his ideas for this book, I knew right away I wanted to be part of it, but I didn't want to horn in on the strength of our friendship. But later, when he asked me if I wanted to do the artwork for it, he got an answer faster than a hobo turns his socks.

Like Mark, I've seen many a good horse ruined by well-meaning, but unknowing people. So this book is a labor of love for me, just as it is for Mark. If, between us, we can cause even one horse owner to get to know his horse better and give them both a better life, then this project has been worth all the effort it took to put it together. I'm proud to be asked to participate in my good buddy's effort and hope that my pictures truly convey his meaning to readers. If everyone who reads this book enjoys it as much as I have, we won't be able to print enough of them.

Ron Ball
Lazy Easel Ranch
Estes Park, Colorado

Special thanks

As with any undertaking of this nature, there is no way it could have been accomplished without the support of good friends and loving family. It is for that reason that I take the opportunity to thank them all personally, and I hope I don't leave anybody out.

Thanks to my parents, Jed and Joan, for the support and guidance they supplied to me as a child, as well as the freedom to choose my own course in life, even when it may not have seemed the best way to go. Thanks to my sisters, Mary and Pam, and my brothers, Rick, Scott, and Craig, for believing in me. Thanks to my in-laws Gordon and Aleene for their help and support when I know it couldn't have been easy to give.

Thanks to Scott and Julie Roederer, who not only asked if I would write this book, but who are also the big reason it has become a reality.

Thanks to Matt Bowers, who got me started writing in the first place and gave me the encouragement to want to continue.

Thanks to Dwight and Jean Thorson, Ron and Jane Ball, Joy York, Patty Lyons, Justin Smith, Scott Bottoms, Linda Goad, Steve and Evelyn Wilson, Linda Wilenski, Dr. Dave and Jill Schneider, Rick Harris, Dennis Clymer, Rob and Jere Irvin, Cathy Irvin, Bob and Cheryl Clifton, Herb and Sherry Mignery, Larry Kitchen, Randy Good, Steve and Gay Nagl, Susie Bail, Fran Vess, George and Jill Pratt, Pat Spivey, Bob Merkins, and Boyd LaMarsh for their friendship and support in both good times and bad.

Thanks to Dr. Rick Dill, D.V.M., and Dr. Dave Siemens for fixing my animals when they needed it.

And a very special thanks to the "old man" for giving me the matches that started the fire and the fuel to keep it burning.

What I found was a big palomino gelding who didn't like to be caught, groomed, saddled, bridled, or ridden. At first glance the problems appeared insurmountable. But after spending a little time with both him and the owners, it became clear that what was going on was more a case of a series of misunderstandings rather than out and out bad behavior by the horse. With a few adjustments on everybody's part, and within a relatively short period of time, all three were getting along much better and the couple decided not to sell the horse after all. Little did I know at the time but that evening would set my life off on a path I could never have imagined.

It turned out that the husband was an editor for a publishing company and after seeing the kind of quiet work we had done with his horse, he asked if I had ever thought about writing a book about what I do. I told him I hadn't and figured that was that. However, one night a few weeks later he called and asked again if I'd be interested in writing a book. During our phone conversation I got to thinking about opportunities, and how certain opportunities don't come around very often. Getting asked to write a book seemed to be one of those. So that night, after a two-hour phone conversation, the idea for *Considering the Horse* was born.

Less than a year later the book came out in print and I suppose like any new author, I looked forward to seeing the finished product. I must say, however, that I was surprised to find that the book was actually a little difficult for me to read. At first, I didn't understand why, but the deeper I got into it the more I realized I had not only lived through the stories in the book, but then wrote the stories down, gone over them several times during the editing process, and then read them again after the editing process and before the manuscript went into publication. By the time the book actually came out I found I just didn't want to go over the stories again. It was as if by rereading the stories over and over I was somehow keeping myself in the past and it didn't take long to realize that staying in the past just wasn't a good place for me to be. In order for me to grow as a person and a horseman I needed to be moving forward, so I put the book down and didn't pick it up again for nearly twenty years.

Now the interesting thing, at least for me, is that during that same twenty years I have had countless people from all over the world send me letters, emails, call me on the phone, or come and see us when we're doing our clinics and tell me how much *Considering the Horse* has meant to them, or how much it has helped them and their horses. I've even had people recite certain stories from the book almost verbatim or tell me how much they laughed or how much they cried during a specific chapter or story. Still, I had that little nagging feeling in the back of my mind that perhaps the information I tried to pass along might have become outdated somehow over time. After all, within just a few years after its publication

I noticed I was already thinking about certain things I wrote about a little differently, other things I was doing differently, and still others I wasn't really doing anymore at all!

Then, a few years back I received a letter from a twelve-year-old girl who told me how much the book meant to her and how much it helped her with her relationship with her horses. She said she had been treating her horses badly for a long time, but didn't know it until she read the book. She went on to say that since reading *Considering the Horse*, she was not only treating her horses with more understanding and kindness, but she was now treating every horse she came in contact with the same way and was finding that being around horses was fun again, where before it was turning into something she hated.

It was then that I began to look at this little book in a different light. I started to understand that while I may see and do things a little differently with horses than I did when the book first came out, the information in the book wasn't outdated at all. I began to understand that the book is a snapshot of where I was in both my life and my horsemanship at that time, and while I feel I am still evolving and moving forward in both, there are also people and horses out there who are still benefitting from reading about the experiences I tried to share in those pages all those years ago.

I finally began to realize that this book has helped a lot of people and horses all over the world, not to mention it was the starting point for what would ultimately turn into a nearly twenty-year-long career of writing for me.

Then in 2005, the publishing company I had worked so closely with for so many years was taken over by a much larger company. Even though all my books were still selling well, the bigger parent company chose to let them go out of print. It started with *A Good Horse Is Never a Bad Color*, in 2008, followed by *Horses Never Lie*, and finally *Considering the Horse*. When Skyhorse Publishing (the publisher of *Whole Heart, Whole Horse*) heard about this, they quickly picked up the rights, and plans immediately began for the reissue of the books, including any updates or additions to the text that I would like to make.

Although *A Good Horse* had been out of print for the longest period of time, we ultimately decided to rerelease them in their original order, beginning with *Considering the Horse*. As result, I started going through the book to see what, if any additions, needed to be made, and I was pleasantly surprised to find that this time, reading it felt like reuniting with an old friend that I hadn't seen in twenty years. The people, places, and horses I wrote about back then jumped off the page at me and came back to life, and while there were indeed things I would add or talk about differently today, I just couldn't bring myself to change any of the original text.

I mentioned earlier that for me this book is like a snapshot in time, and I quickly found changing or adding to the original text would have been like trying to "photoshop" a favorite old photograph—doing so may make the photo look better or different, but it wouldn't make it the original. So instead of adding or subtracting to the original text, I simply decided to put any changes, additions, or thoughts I might have had about something I wrote about back in 1992 at the end of the chapter in question. You'll notice, as you read through, that some chapters have very little at the end of them, while others have more extensive additions. Please keep in mind that none of the additions or comments were meant as a discussion on specifically how I do things now, as my subsequent books have most of that information in them already.

As I mentioned at the outset, I felt back then, and still do today that getting a chance to write this book was a once in a lifetime opportunity. After all, very few people ever get asked to write a book in the first place, and it seems even fewer get the opportunity to add to it nearly twenty years later. I've been lucky enough to be able to do both, and it's been a privilege and an honor to get the chance to do so. I have you, the reader to thank for that.

As one might imagine, working on this project was truly a labor of love back in 1992. In many ways, it was even more so now. So for those of you "old timers" who had a chance to read the book in its original form, I hope you like the additions we chose to add. For those newcomers who are just picking the book up for the first time . . . welcome, and I hope you enjoy reading it as much as I've enjoyed bringing it to you.

Mark Rashid
2010

Part One

Horse Sense

to rebuild but ended up going broke and selling the place to Jim Johnson ten years later. Johnson wanted the place to raise, train, and sell horses.

The first thing that Johnson noticed about the place was the one power line pole that the tornado didn't get. It was planted firmly next to the southwest corner of the tool shed and hadn't been used for its original purpose since the storm. It was, he thought, the perfect piece of wood to use for the snubbing post that he wanted in the middle of the round pen he planned on building. With picks and shovels, he and his uncle tried to dig the pole up.

Two days later, and with the pole still in the ground, they decided it would be easier to build the round pen around the pole rather than move the pole to the round pen. So that's what they did.

They tore down the tool shed and built the round pen there. The sides of the round pen were angled out slightly and built out of rough-cut 2 × 12s. The top board was six feet, six inches off the ground and was used mainly as a place for people to sit and watch the horses being broke. The round pen had gotten so much use over the years that the floor was nothing but a mixture of dirt and pulverized horse manure.

In the wet season, this combination rendered the round pen virtually unusable. The floor would become so slick that it was literally impossible to walk across, much less work horses in. Using it in the dry season wasn't much better. Working horses in the pen would raise so much dust that people passing by often mistook the dust cloud for smoke from a burning building.

It was on one of those dry, dusty days in the summer of 1968 that I found myself sitting on the top board of the Johnson round pen. Sitting next to me was Walter Pruit, my boss. We had driven the four miles or so from Walter's horse ranch to Johnson's to pick up a truckload of hay and, having already loaded the truck, had stopped to watch the boys work one of the new colts.

It was the first time I had ever gotten to see a horse being broke close up, and I was so excited that I could hardly sit still. Through the dust I could see them work. One of the men had a foot braced against the old power pole in the middle of the pen. He did this to get leverage on the rope he was holding, which was wrapped two or three times around the pole. On the other end of the rope was a heavy leather halter, which was around the head of the colt, and the colt was blindfolded with a towel.

The second man had one hand on the towel, and the other on the horse's ear, which he appeared to be pulling with all his might. He also had his teeth clamped down on the end of the same ear. The third man was working as fast as he could to cinch up the saddle that he had just thrown on the horse's back.

All three men were sweating so much that the dust that hit them immediately turned to mud. Their arms and faces were streaked with the dark slippery stuff, and their shirts were so covered that it was hard to tell what color they were when put on that morning.

This was an awesome display of horsemanship, I thought. There was no question that this horse had met its match. As I sat there watching, I kept thinking that someday this was what I wanted to do—break horses.

Other ranch hands had also begun to gather around and were shouting encouragement to the three horsemen in the pen. I found myself shouting with them. As the third man was getting ready to get on, something strange happened. I heard the soft voice of the old man sitting next to me.

"How do you suppose the horse feels about all this?" he asked quietly, putting a filterless Camel cigarette between his lips and lighting it.

"What?" I asked, over the cheers of the crowd.

"The horse." He blew out a puff of bluish smoke. "How do you think the horse feels about this?"

"It's just a horse," I heard my twelve-year-old voice say, almost in disgust.

To me at that point, horses were simply objects to be overpowered and pushed around. Giving consideration as to how the horse felt never entered my mind. Of course, nobody had ever asked me to consider it either, until that day.

I turned my attention back to the action just in time to see the cowboy throw a leg over the horse and take a deep seat. Suddenly, and for the first time, I noticed the horse. She was soaked with sweat and dirt, which made determining her exact color impossible. She stood snubbed to the post in the dust and heat. Every muscle in her body was rigid and quivering with fear. As the man pulled the blindfold off and turned her loose, the expression on her face was unmistakably one of terror.

The rider, ready for action, hooked the little mare with his spurs. She quickly exploded in a blur of hooves, hair, and dust. She bucked so hard and fast that as her back legs reached their full extension, they made a popping sound. The bellarin' sound that she made as the air was forced out of her lungs with every jump was awful. I had never heard that exact sound before, or since.

I heard one of the boys who was sitting on the top rail with us comment that Tony, the man on the horse's back, had bit off more than he could chew, and evidently he had. Horse and rider made only three very fast and furious laps around the round pen before Tony was launched into the air like that guy I'd once seen at the county fair who shot himself out of the cannon. Tony landed in a heap about twenty feet from where he came off. As men scrambled into the round pen to help him and to try to catch the horse, the old man nudged my arm.

How do you suppose the horse feels about all this?

"Come on," he said, throwing a leg over the back side of the round pen. "We've got hay to unload."

I had worked on the old man's little horse operation since I was ten years old, mostly as a poop scooper and gofer. In exchange I was able to ride for free. During those two years, I had gone with the "old man" about a half dozen times to pick up hay. While loading the hay, I would stand on the stack and throw the bales down onto the truck where he would stack them. The truck was a 1949 Ford pickup that looked like it had rolled off a cliff somewhere and, by some stroke of luck, had landed on its wheels still running.

The old man would always insist on stacking about five more bales on the truck than it could carry. He then would refuse to tie the stack to the bed proclaiming that we didn't have that far to go and tying the stack would waste time. Inevitably we would dump nearly the entire load in the middle of the road on the way home. We would then have to spend at least another hour putting the bales back on the truck.

This day was no exception. As we rounded the corner out of Johnson's driveway onto the main road, I felt the telltale lurch of the truck that told me that the hay bales that were once on the back were now in the road.

The entire time we were reloading the truck, the only thing I could think of was that question he asked me at the round pen: how did I suppose the horse felt about all of that? It was as if, with that one question, the old man had tried to open my eyes to another side of horses that many people, including myself at that point, never see. I wanted to let him know that I understood what he was trying to get at. I also wanted to let him know that I'd seen in the horse what he had seen—the fear.

The problem was, as the two of us stood there stacking hay on that pickup, I just couldn't find the words. Nothing I could think of seemed appropriate. It wasn't until the second-to-last bale was being tossed on the truck that I said something.

"She was scared," I told him apologetically.

The old man stopped and looked at me as if to say, "I don't know what you're talking about," although I knew he did.

"The horse," I continued. "She was scared. That's how she felt."

He nodded his head approvingly and said quietly, "I'm glad you noticed." I waited for him to say something more. Perhaps something profound like, "All good horsemen notice those things." Or, "You're very observant." Or even, "You're not as stupid as I thought you were." But nothing else was said.

As time went on, I came to realize that nothing else needed to be said. He had gotten his point across. The point was that there is more to horses than simply getting on and riding—a lot more. He had made his point, and the rest was up to me. I could either do something about it or let it go. I decided from that day on to make more of an effort to find out just what makes horses tick.

Now, I wish I could say that the rest of that summer was a tremendous learning experience for me. It wasn't. Although I was now trying to look at horses from a different perspective, the truth of the matter is, things went on pretty much the way they always had with me scooping poop and fixing fence and seldom if ever actually working with the horses.

It wasn't until the following spring that I was able to put my newfound attitude towards horses to work. One morning as I was cleaning stalls, a pickup with a stock trailer pulled into the yard. Inside the trailer was a sorrel gelding that was throwing himself around in an attempt to get out. The driver backed the trailer up to one of the empty corrals where the old man had opened the gate. No sooner had they opened the back door of the trailer than the gelding leaped into the 20-by-30-foot corral and hit the ground running. He quickly found that there wasn't anywhere to go, however, and planted himself in the corner farthest away from everybody.

He had several superficial cuts on his head, legs, and hips and was shaking so badly from fear that I thought he might tip over. The driver of the truck said the horse was just plain worthless, and if we could train him, we could have him. As the trailer pulled away, the old man came over to where I was, which was next to the corral fence.

"Do you want to work with this one?" he asked matter-of-factly. The old man had never before even hinted that I might someday be able to work with the horses, so the question took me by complete surprise.

"I wouldn't know what to do with him," I said.

"That horse will show you what to do," was his reply. "Just look at everything you do from his point of view, and the rest will take care of itself."

"I wouldn't even know where to start," I told him.

"He's scared," the old man grunted. "That's where you start." And he walked off.

There it was. Again, he had left it up to me. I could either take the bull by the horns and work with this horse or go back to cleaning stalls. Having weighed my options carefully, and not wanting to rush into anything, I went back to cleaning stalls. For two days I went about my business as usual. Then on the third day I heard the old man holler for me from his pickup truck. He told me over the noise of the engine that he had to go to town. He also said that somehow a halter had gotten in the new gelding's pen and would I go in and get it. I told him I would.

The familiar sound of banging metal and grinding gears faded into the distance as I rounded the corner to the gelding's pen. I was shocked to see that the only halter in the pen was buckled around the horse's neck. That morning the old man had somehow gotten close enough to that horse not only to catch him but to put the halter on him. He had even done it without me seeing or hearing him. I couldn't believe it. Well, I thought to myself as only a teenager can, if he can do it, I can do it.

With all the grit and determination I could muster, I entered the pen. The horse was not impressed. He simply turned and began to trot around the perimeter of the corral. Dauntlessly I followed him. Fifteen minutes later the situation hadn't changed. He was still trotting, and I was still following.

Twenty-five minutes went by before I decided to rethink my strategy. I moved to the center of the corral and stood so as to catch my breath. Much to my surprise, the horse stopped too. Not only that, but he turned and looked at me as well.

We had both stood motionless looking at each other for quite some time, each trying to figure out what to do next, when I noticed a bee flying in my direction. It was one of those bees which have black-and-yellow bodies the size of fifty-five-gallon drums and which sound like a Peterbilt as they fly past. The bee ended up right in front of me, about chest high and hovering. I decided to take some evasive action by moving a few steps backwards.

The bee flew around my head three or four times and again hovered in front of me about chest high. Again I stepped back. We had done this three more times when the bee decided the fun was over and flew off. My full attention had been on the bee, so when I finally was able to return my attention to the horse, I was surprised to see that he had moved to the center of the pen. I had backed away from the center because of the bee and was now standing closer to the fence.

It suddenly occurred to me that as I was backing away, the horse might have been following me, much the same as I'd been following him as he was moving away from me. Wanting to see if this was indeed the case, I took a couple more steps backwards. The horse hesitated, then took a couple of steps forward, towards me.

It was a revelation. The more I thought about it, the more sense it made. If I were scared and somebody were chasing me, I'd run away. That was exactly what the horse had been doing, running away from me because I was scaring him. When I stopped following him, his fear started to go away, and he felt comfortable enough to stop. The one thing I couldn't figure out was why he had decided to start following me. While that puzzled me, I didn't spend much time dwelling on it. At least he wasn't running away any more. The fact that he was making an effort to get close to me was simply a bonus.

I continued to back away, and he continued to follow. He was also getting closer to me with each step. Ten minutes later, he was standing with his head less than a foot from

We had both stood motionless looking at each other.

my chest. I slowly brought my hand up and touched his nose. He acted a little nervous but didn't run off. I lowered my hand and tried again. He seemed to accept it a little better but still acted scared.

I continued on, touching him and then lowering my hand. I did that for quite some time, it seemed, before I was actually able to pet him on his forehead, nose, and cheeks. I remember being so afraid to make a mistake or do something that might frighten him that all of my movements had become painfully slow. As it turned out, all of that slow movement was just what he needed. It seemed to have an overwhelmingly calming effect on him. By handling him in such a way, I was able to work my way around to his side and consequently take the halter from around his neck.

Having taken the halter off, I backed away from the horse and headed for the gate. I was beside myself. I felt that the horse had willingly allowed me to remove the halter, even though he was afraid. I had tried to put myself in his place and did what I thought would make me comfortable in a similar situation. It worked.

I couldn't wait for the old man to get back so I could describe my feat to him. When he finally did return, he sat quietly on a hay bale smoking a cigarette and listening intently as I rambled on and on in great detail about exactly how I was able to remove the halter.

"Sounds like you did everything just right," he said, when I finally let him get a word in edgewise. "It wasn't as tough as you thought, was it?"

"No!" I chimed back. "It was great."

The old man nodded his head slowly, took a drag on his cigarette, and said, "Well, better get back to work. We still got stalls to clean."

Stalls, I thought. How could he possibly ask me to clean stalls? After all, I had gotten the halter off! Evidently getting the halter off that horse wasn't as big a deal to him as it was to me. But it didn't matter. I had done it, and no one could ever take that away from me. Besides, for me, it was a beginning. I had heard the old man talk about the horse's point of view countless times, and although I didn't understand it, at least I'd seen it. Understanding it would come in time.

Over the next few years, I began to develop a working knowledge of training horses from their point of view. This is similar to a one-legged man saying he has a working knowledge of square dancing. He may be able to do the dance, but it's not as pretty as it could be.

I began to realize that if I wanted to be any good at this or any other type of training, I'd need to do two things. First, learn as much about the horse, as an animal, as I could. And second, get my hands on as many horses as possible. This way I could apply to the horses, on an individual basis, the information I had learned. The problem was that much of the information that I was picking up, either through books or firsthand information from other horse people, wasn't coinciding with what I'd learned from the old man and what the horses themselves were telling me.

For instance, it is generally believed that horses are not very intelligent animals and are unable to reason. However, by working with horses on a daily basis, I saw just the opposite. I saw horses that had taught themselves how to open gates. Others, knowing they'd be cinched too tight, would bloat; then, they would let the air out when the rider was on so that they'd be comfortable while being ridden. I saw other horses that would be either easy or hard to catch, depending on how they were going to be treated once caught.

Many people who have these types of things happen with their horses think the horses are born troublemakers, simply because they're doing something that the person thinks is wrong or undesirable. However, the one thing that I have come to understand about horses is that they're not like people. They don't think like we do and they don't learn like we do. It is when we try to force the animal to live by human thoughts, feelings, and emotions that we run into trouble.

What we often forget is when a horse is born, any horse, all it knows to be is a horse. Not the trained, domesticated horse that stands in your backyard, but a wild animal, the kind that lives on pure instinct. This particular animal's first instinct of survival is to get away from anything that scares him, and until he knows different, everything scares him. It's that one element in the horse's total make-up that will control him from the day he's born until the day he dies. It is also what is most misunderstood about him. Because the horse doesn't respond the way we think he should, he is deemed stupid or worthless. In reality he may simply be responding the only way his mind will let him, by trying to survive or protect himself.

This one simple element became painfully evident to me the summer before the old man died. He had turned a horse over to me that he said had been beat up some and was a little spooky. He wanted me to see if I could get him to settle down enough to be ridden.

By the time I got this horse, I had successfully trained or retrained about a dozen head. Because of these successes, it would be safe to say that I was feeling just a little bit cocky. I had followed pretty much the same training schedule with each of the twelve previous horses. A couple of days in the round pen getting to know one another, two or three days longeing and ground driving, a day or two working with the horse getting used to the saddle, and finally I was on and riding around. I had no reason to think that this horse would be any different.

I was surprised to see, however, that after the first three days in the round pen, there wasn't much change in the horse's attitude. The two days that we worked on longeing and ground driving weren't any better and, in some ways, were actually worse. It didn't matter, though, because after the seven days that I had allotted this horse, I was able to get the saddle on him and even put weight in the stirrups.

On the eighth day, I threw a leg over and sat quietly in the saddle. He was shaking with fear, and I tried to calm him by petting him on his neck. Looking back, it must have been like trying to put out a forest fire with a squirt gun. Again, it didn't matter at the time—at least I was on him.

After I'd been on him for several minutes, I decided to ask him to move forward by bumping him three times lightly with my heels. The only response I got was a fearful jerking of his entire body each time my heels hit him. Because he hadn't responded the way I thought he should, I decided to put a little more pressure on him. I did this by giving him one sharp, hard kick.

Now, I have always been amazed at how much explosive energy a horse can muster when he really wants to get whoever is on his back, off. Especially when that person has been a source of stress and aggravation to him for over a week.

This particular horse unloaded me so fast that I was face first in the dirt before I even realized I was in trouble. I remember spitting out a barrage of cuss words that peeled the paint off the barn. Some of those words I didn't even know the meaning of. As I picked myself up off the ground, I faced the horse and yelled, "Stupid, damn, worthless horse!" at the top of my lungs.

Just then I noticed the old man leaning on the corral fence staring at me with that look on his face. The look that told me that the whole thing was my fault to begin with for trying to make that horse fit a preconceived notion of how he should behave. Of course, he was right. Because of my impatience with the horse, I had left him no alternative but to defend himself from what he perceived as a threat. His survival instinct had taken over, and as a result, I ended up with a face full of dirt. They call that poetic justice, I think.

The point I'm trying to make is that I don't believe horses are stupid. In fact, I think that they may be a whole lot more intelligent than we give them credit for. We just perceive them as not being very smart, because when things start to go wrong or they become confused, their instincts take over. When this happens, they appear to us to do stupid things or, at least, things that don't make any sense. To horses, however, their reactions may simply mean the difference between life and death.

I remember the old man telling me that if I wanted to be a good trainer, I'd have to stop thinking like a person and start thinking like a horse. I needed to try to see the world through the horse's eyes, not mine. That has proven to be easier said than done for me, even though it's the attitude that I literally grew up with.

I have found that along with understanding why the horse acts and reacts the way he does, I have also had to develop a tremendous amount of patience. There are several reasons for this, but I think the most important is that horses do not know how to tell time. What I mean by this is that, unlike us, horses are never under any time constraints. They don't have to do the shopping, they don't go to movies, they don't have to do the banking or laundry, they don't even "do lunch."

In other words, they have all day to learn what we're trying to teach. It doesn't matter to them if we have to be somewhere at three o'clock. They don't. They cannot be forced into understanding or doing something faster just because we're running out of time. This in itself is probably the biggest reason why people have problems with their horses. This and the fact that many people seem to have an inherent need to dominate and intimidate horses, more than a willingness to communicate with them.

I remember working as a volunteer for a benefit trail ride in early September some years ago. As is often the case in the foothills of Colorado during the early fall, the temperature had risen into the mid-nineties, and there wasn't a cloud in the sky. It was a fifteen-mile ride that began around eight in the morning and ended around two o'clock.

The parking lot of the trailhead where the ride began and ultimately finished was filled with horse trailers of all makes, shapes, and sizes. In one corner of the lot stood a pickup with a very nice, dark gray, two-horse trailer attached. The back doors of the trailer were split, each having a bottom and top that, when shut, allowed the trailer to be completely enclosed, which it had been all day.

When the trail ride was finished, a woman on a very flashy, bay quarter horse gelding rode up to the trailer. She dismounted, tied the horse to the trailer, pulled off his tack, and began to meticulously groom him. By that time, the temperature had reached ninety-seven degrees.

As she finished grooming the horse, she untied him, walked him to the back of the trailer, and opened the doors. Heat rushed out of the trailer like it was an oversized pizza oven. It was so intense that the woman had to back away, fanning her face with her hand as she went. She waited about thirty seconds, then led the horse up to the door and asked him to load. He put his head and one foot in the trailer, then immediately backed out. He looked at the woman as if to say, "Boy, it's real hot in there. How about we wait a few minutes before I get in?"

The woman ignored him. She led the horse back to the trailer and asked him to load again. The gelding balked, and the fight was on. For the next two hours, a tremendous battle was waged between the human being's sometimes violent nature and the horse's instinct to keep himself alive. At one point, I counted seventeen people standing around the horse and trailer, each offering their advice and muscle. None were successful.

Over that same two-hour period, I had several times overheard the horse's owner mention that she had to be home by five o'clock because she had dinner guests coming. Now, because of her "stupid" horse not loading, she was going to be late. I found it interesting that she would blame the result of her impatience on her horse, a horse that, by her own admission, had never before hesitated to load. I also couldn't help thinking that, had she taken ten or fifteen minutes to let the trailer air out in the first place, she could have avoided the entire incident.

Instead, she made the same mistake I'd made with the horse that had planted me in the dirt. She had tried to force her horse into doing something quicker than he was prepared to do it. The end result was the same. His survival instinct had taken over, and he went into a self-defense mode. As this defensive mode intensified, it became clear that the woman could have had every person in the city of Denver there to help, and that horse still wouldn't have gotten into that trailer. His instincts had overridden all of his training and were telling him that he was in a life-threatening situation, even though he wasn't.

Over the years I have come to realize that nearly every training problem that horses develop stems from our lack of understanding of this simple point of view. When this is coupled with the fact that we are often in too much of a hurry to get the animal to perform what we're asking, training sessions and trail rides often end in disaster.

I can't help but compare the way some people work with horses to the way that the old man hauled hay. He didn't want to take the extra fifteen minutes to tie a load to the truck, so we would end up spending over an hour reloading the thing after the hay had fallen off. It's basically the same with horses. If we don't take the time to do it right the first time, we will most certainly have to take the time to do it over. I have seen too many good horses become problem horses due simply to our lack of understanding and willingness to find a way to communicate with them, when, with a little patience and effort on our part, the problems would have been avoided altogether.

Of course, I'm certainly not trying to imply that understanding the horse's point of view will make training them simple and easy. It's not that cut-and-dried. It also takes a mindset that is completely contrary to the old-time, rough-and-tumble, cowboy way of breaking horses. It means a soft hand instead of a big stick—a tough idea for some people to take hold of.

I recall visiting the old Johnson place in the summer of 1980, only days before it was to be bulldozed to make way for some new condos. The place had been abandoned since 1975 when Jim Johnson died, and it stuck out like a sore thumb in the middle of what was now suburbia.

I made my way through the hip-high weeds to the old dilapidated round pen, climbed to the top board, and sat down. I gazed past the combination of weeds and alfalfa plants that had somehow managed to grow inside the pen, to the old power pole that still stood in the middle. Just inches above the tops of the weeds were scars of the pole's many battles with the horses that had been snubbed to it. Three separate indentations an inch or more deep had been made by the hundreds of ropes used to snub horses to the pole.

I've often thought of how some people's attitudes towards horse training are a lot like that old pole—unyielding and unforgiving and buried so deep that you can't get them out. I've also thought about all the horses that never stood a chance against it, and the attitude that brought it into use in the first place.

However, at the same time, I also realize that many horse owners simply don't know any better. They handle horses the way they've been taught and have never been introduced to any other way of handling them. Just like me, they will never know the difference if someone doesn't make the effort to show them, or they don't make the effort to find it. It has been my experience that most horse owners, when they realize that horses do indeed have a point of view, try to make an effort to work with the animal, instead of against it.

Old attitudes can be changed. Sometimes it simply takes a little more effort and time than we'd originally thought. Just like that old pole that stood dauntless in the middle of the round pen all those years. It finally came down. It's just that it took an eight-ton bulldozer to do it.

NOTES FOR THE HORSE'S POINT OF VIEW

In this chapter I introduce for the first time the old friend and mentor from my childhood who took me under his wing and began to slowly, and even painfully at times, show me about horses. I really struggled with how much to include stories about him before I started writing the book because I wasn't sure how many people would be interested in hearing about something that happened nearly thirty years in the past. As it turned out, however, my worry was for nothing. "The old man" is the one person people never seemed to get enough of, and I found in my subsequent books if I didn't include enough stories about him, they would let me know about it!

Anywhere I go in the world, people always ask me about him and I thought this might be a good time to answer a few of those frequently asked questions.

Q. Was there really an "old man"?

A. Yes. As I explain in several of my books, he owned a little horse operation not far from where I lived and I spent quite a bit of time with him starting when I was around ten years old, and continuing off and on until I was about fifteen.

Q. Was he Tom Dorrance?

A. No.

Q. What was "the old man's" name?

A. I do mention his name in each of my books where I tell stories about him, but people seem to miss it. His name, as far as I remember, was Walter Pruit. I say as far as I remember because while I heard his first name mentioned numerous times over the years, I only recall hearing his last name a time or two. Pruit is the name I vaguely remember, but it could easily have been something else, or something that sounded like Pruit. Still, I have always believed it to be Pruit, so that is the name I used when talking about him.

Q. I imagine him to look a certain way. What did he really look like?

A. Other than mentioning that he smoked a lot, and from time to time the types of clothes he wore, I never mention specifically what he looked like. I did this for a reason. I felt that if his personality resonated with people, I wanted them to form their own picture of him in their mind . . . someone they might be comfortable with if the things I was writing about were actually happening to them. So in each of my books, starting with this one, I intentionally left out a full description of him, and it is my belief that part of the reason so many do resonate with him is because the picture they have of him wasn't predetermined for them.

Problem causes

"I've got to go look at a horse," the old man said, as he walked past me. "You want to come along?"

"You bet," I chimed. I leaned my pitchfork up against the wall and jogged behind him as he made his way to the old pickup. When the old man said he had to "look at a horse," it usually meant that he was in the market to buy, and watching him buy horses was always an experience.

He seemed to be a master at knowing an animal's current and potential worth, often by doing no more than talking to the horse's owner over the phone. He also had a knack for convincing the animal's owner to sell it to him for the exact amount that he was willing to pay, without him having to haggle over the price.

It was always great fun to watch him work his horse-trading magic, and I jumped at every opportunity that came along to do so. There was, however, always one obstacle that stood in the way of an immediate departure—the passenger door on the old pickup truck. Before I could get in the truck, I would first have to go through the "passenger door ritual." This consisted of reaching in through the open window, grabbing the inside door handle, and pulling with all my might while at the same time kicking the bottom of the door. Inevitably, the door would burst open, hitting me squarely in the shin and prompting a short but heartfelt one-legged jig on my part.

Once inside the truck, it generally took three or four hearty slams to get the door closed securely. Of course, slamming the door in such a way also disturbed the five or six thousand flies that had taken up residence in the cab of the truck. The only way to get the swarming flies out was to get the truck up to about 40 MPH (a feat in itself), have the windows wide open, and fan our arms wildly. This kept the flies in flight long enough to be caught in the crosswind inside the cab. After about five or six miles, the wind would ultimately suck them all out the windows.

By the time the old man had turned the truck into the driveway of the elaborate boarding stable where the horse was, we had successfully rid the cab of every single fly. The sight and sound of the old Ford was a sharp and distinct contrast to the miles of white fences, meticulously groomed, high-dollar horses, and spotless white and red barns. As we drove in, I couldn't help but feel like the man who arrives at a party thinking it's a masquerade ball, only to find out that it's a $200-per-plate, black-tie dinner.

We pulled up to the second of the three barns, shut off the truck, and got out. We hadn't gotten more than six feet away from the contraption when it let out a very loud and enthusiastic backfire. The old man looked at me with a twinkle in his eye and chuckled.

"Now there's a truck with character," he quipped, as we made our way down the aisle and up to a young woman who had been grooming her thoroughbred gelding. The backfire appeared to have unnerved the horse somewhat.

"Excuse me, ma'am," the old man said politely and as if the frightened horse next to her didn't exist. "Could you please tell me where Mr. John Forms might be?"

"Who?" the woman said, almost yelling as she slapped her horse on the neck, apparently reprimanding him for his behavior.

"John Forms," the old man repeated quietly.

"In the arena, out back," she hissed.

"Thank you," the old man said, tipping his hat, but the woman was too involved with her horse to notice. We continued down the aisle amid the sounds of her cussing and the crashing and banging of the horse as he knocked over first her grooming tools and then a bucket full of oats. The old man seemed completely oblivious to the commotion behind us and, unlike me, never even looked back.

I would first have to go through the "passenger door ritual."

We exited the back door of the barn and came upon a very large, well-maintained outdoor riding arena. In the arena, several horses were being exercised by their riders. For the most part, the horses appeared to be very manageable and well trained—except for one horse in the middle of the arena. He was a very good-looking, dapple-gray gelding and was causing such a commotion that the other riders were doing everything they could to stay out of his way. He was crow hopping, rearing, shaking his head, squealing, snorting, and spinning. And all, it seemed, at the same time.

As we stood there watching, two things were going through my mind. The first was that I couldn't believe the rider was able to stay on, and the second was that I hoped that this wasn't the horse that we'd come to see. If it was, I was sure the old man would deem the outing a waste of time, and we would soon be on our way home, which meant that I'd be back to cleaning stalls.

"Which one are we here to look at?" I asked, as the old man lit up what had to be his twenty-fifth cigarette of the morning.

"The gray," he said matter-of-factly.

Just then, the horse dropped a shoulder, let out with a buck, and the rider was airborne. The man had no sooner hit the ground than he was back on his feet, jerking violently on the reins. He backed the horse nearly the entire length of the arena before trying to get back on.

The horse spun in a quick circle several times, making it next to impossible for the man to get his foot in the stirrup. The man began jerking on the reins once again. This time when he stopped, the horse allowed him to get back on. However, as his butt hit the saddle, the horse suddenly stampeded off across the arena, forcing the other riders to scatter. For the next several minutes we watched as more of the same happened.

I felt myself wince as I said, "It kind of looks like that horse has a problem." I was referring to what appeared to me to be a bad attitude.

The old man took the last drag from his cigarette and dropped it on the ground. "He sure does," he said, mashing the butt with the toe of his boot and leaning against the arena rail. "His rider."

Apparently the old man was seeing something that I wasn't, but not wanting to look like a fool I nodded my head knowingly in agreement.

"Maybe we can get him bought before this guy ruins him completely," he said, climbing over the top rail of the arena. The old man made his way to where the horse and rider were and negotiations for purchasing the animal began. The horse's owner, John Forms, was also his rider. He told the old man that he wanted $750 for him.

"He's not worth that," the old man said bluntly, shaking his head.

"What do you mean?" Forms countered. "This is a good horse. He just has a lot of spirit."

"We've been here for twenty minutes," the old man replied, "and I haven't seen that horse stand with all four feet on the ground at the same time yet." It was true. Even as the two men were talking, the horse couldn't seem to stand still.

"He just has a lot of energy," Forms said, trying to force a smile.

The old man stood with a look on his face that said, "Come on friend—we both know better than that." The two men stood looking at each other and the horse for quite some time before Forms finally asked how much the old man was willing to pay.

"$225," was his reply.

"I can't sell him for that," Forms told him in disgust.

"Okay," the old man said, as if the whole affair couldn't have meant less to him. "Thanks for your time." And with that we turned and walked away.

We had gotten all the way to the truck, and I was in the middle of the passenger door ritual when Forms emerged from the barn and made his way to the old man's door.

"How about $300?" he blurted.

"$225," the old man said. "That's all he's worth."

"$250, and I'll deliver him."

The old man sat with his hands on the steering wheel quietly looking forward as if he were in deep thought. In reality, he was just sitting. What Forms didn't know was that $250 was the exact price the old man was willing to pay to begin with. He'd told me so on the drive over.

After a couple minutes of silence on the old man's part, he finally said, "I guess I could do it for $250 as long as you'll deliver him."

"Good," Forms said. "I can have him at your place this afternoon."

"Done," the old man replied with a smile, offering his hand. The handshake sealed the deal, and later that day the horse was at the old man's place.

A couple of days later, I arrived at work to see the old man riding the gray out in one of the pastures. Had I not known any better, I wouldn't have believed that it was the same horse. The horse was quiet and responsive, not only in the walk but the trot and lope as well.

The old man saw me and rode over. As he approached, he gently asked the horse to stop by leaning slightly backwards and quietly picking up on the reins. The horse stopped in mid-stride and immediately relaxed with his head down.

"Well," he said dropping the reins over the horse's neck so he could light a cigarette. "What do you think?"

"How did you get him to be so quiet?" I said, shaking my head in disbelief.

"I didn't get him to do anything," he replied. "This has been a quiet horse all along. His owner just wasn't allowing him to be."

He went on to explain that horses don't act as bad as this one had without a reason. This horse's reason was that his owner was so heavy-handed that he had given the horse no alternative but to defend himself whenever the man was around. In other words, he wasn't giving the horse the opportunity to be good. The horse's response was fearful nervousness and apparent uncontrollability. The owner's response was to sell him before he got himself killed.

"My job," the old man smiled, "is to buy horses like this, straighten them out, and sell them for a profit."

"But if the man doesn't know he's doing something wrong," I questioned, "how will he ever be able to correct himself?"

"He won't," the old man replied. "And I'll make money off his horses for the rest of my life."

"Wouldn't it make more sense to help the man learn how not to make the mistakes, instead of having him ruin horse after horse?" I asked.

"I'll tell you a secret about people," he said, leaning on his saddle horn. "You can't help somebody who doesn't want to be helped, especially when it comes to them and their horses."

As I walked into the barn to start my chores, it suddenly came to me what he was talking about. In all the time I'd known the old man, I had never once seen him offer advice to anybody on how they should be handling their horse, even when the slightest bit of information from him could have helped tremendously. It was the same reason why he had ignored the thoroughbred that was acting up in the barn at the boarding stable. The woman didn't ask for his help to settle the horse down, so he offered none. In order for her to have asked for help, she first had to admit that she was perhaps doing something wrong. Most people don't like to admit that and will often take offense when help is offered. So, instead of running the risk of offending the woman and in turn perhaps making things even worse for the horse, he simply did nothing at all.

On the other hand, I had seen people ask the old man for his help, and it was like opening the floodgates. Information would pour out of him like water through a broken dam, and both horse and rider became better for it. However, if they didn't ask, he didn't offer. He simply bought the horses that were ruined, fixed the problems, and resold them. Just like the gray. He turned around three weeks after buying it and sold it to a young woman for $750. A $500 profit in three weeks' time, and an expensive price for the horse's previous owner to have paid for being ignorant in his own horsemanship skills.

Since those early days with the old man, I guess I've seen hundreds and possibly thousands of horse owners in the same boat—having horses that they can't get along with simply because they don't know how. Then, instead of looking for help, they try to muddle through the problems, dealing with the animal like it was a problem child or disgruntled employee, instead of like a confused horse.

For the longest time I was a firm believer that nearly all problems that horses develop were caused in such a way. However, as the years pass, I have come to realize that this is not always the case. I remember getting a phone call one night from a woman who was having problems with her horse. She said that she had owned the horse for less than three months, and when she bought the mare, the horse was very well trained, quiet, and friendly. But now she was terribly hard to catch, would pull back when tied, was hard to saddle and bridle, and was on the brink of being uncontrollable when being ridden. These are all classic signs of a horse that is being handled improperly or a horse owner who has more horse than he or she can handle.

I agreed to have a look at the horse and see if we could figure out what was causing the behavior and then try to fix the problems. Two days later, on one of the hottest days of the summer, I found myself driving out on the eastern plains of Colorado. So far east, in fact, that I was afraid I might end up in Kansas.

Between leaning forward to peel my sweat-soaked shirt from the truck seat and watching the truck's temperature gauge, which was threatening to go into the red zone, I tried to recall our phone conversation of two nights earlier. I was fairly certain that this would be just another horse owner who had gotten herself in over her head by thinking she was a better horseperson than she was. But still, something was bothering me.

Her voice on the phone was quiet, friendly, and cheerful, and she was very open to suggestions. She also seemed very knowledgeable about horses and genuinely concerned that she may be causing the problems. She wanted to fix whatever it was that she was doing wrong as soon as possible, so as not to put the horse through any more discomfort. These things didn't seem to fit the mold of a person who unknowingly was causing her horse's problems.

After nearly two-and-a-half hours on the road, I finally arrived at the boarding stable where the mare was being kept. I was surprised at the number of horses being boarded there, considering its location, and at the number of people there that day, considering the heat.

I climbed out of the truck and immediately took my felt hat off and replaced it with a baseball cap, which hopefully would prove to be cooler. I had no sooner done that when an attractive young lady approached and introduced herself as the person who had called me.

"Where's our little mare at?" I asked, following the introduction.

"Out in pasture. Shall we go get her?"

"You bet," I said, trying to pretend like it wasn't 104 degrees in the shade.

As we walked the short distance to the pasture gate, we filled the time with small talk. I also noticed as we were walking how some of the other boarders were handling their horses. It appeared that four of the seven people who had their horses out, either riding, longeing, or grooming, were spending an awful lot of energy reprimanding them.

One horse that was being groomed at one of the hitch rails offered to nibble on the rail, apparently out of boredom, as his owner carried on a lengthy conversation with a couple of other boarders. The horse's owner walked over and whacked the horse squarely on the jaw with a curry comb, while at the same time yelling, "Knock it off!" The horse immediately pulled back, frightening the two other horses tied to the same rail.

In the arena, a fellow was jerking mercilessly on his horse's mouth while riding, forcing the animal to rear and spin. The man in the round pen was free-longeing his horse by constantly hitting its back legs with a long longe whip. And one woman, for reasons that I couldn't figure out, was jerking her horse around by a chain looped over the bridge of its nose.

As the woman and I made our way out into the pasture, she pointed out her horse, a buckskin mare, that of course had to be grazing, along with several other horses, in the farthest reaches of the pasture.

"She's been pretty hard to catch lately," the woman said with a halfhearted smile. "Maybe I should get some grain."

As a rule, I don't like to catch horses by bribing them with grain or other treats, but standing there in that blazing sun with sweat running down the middle of my back and more sweat dripping off the end of my nose, bribery suddenly didn't seem like such a bad idea.

"That may be the way to go," I agreed. "I'll wait here." She returned a short time later with a bucket half full of sweet feed.

"This usually brings them pretty quickly," she said, shaking the bucket.

In the distance, I could see their heads come up in response to the sound of the grain. One by one, each of the eleven head grazing in the pasture began to make their way towards us, first at a walk, then a trot, and finally a lope. After going only a short distance in the lope, they dropped back to a trot, and then a walk, as if to say, "It's too damn hot to run, even if they do have grain."

She dumped the grain on the ground in several small piles as the horses reached us, and we were able to catch her mare with little difficulty. She spoke very softly to the little buckskin as she slipped the halter over her nose and buckled it in place. The horse seemed very quiet and relaxed as we stood there talking.

"She doesn't look too bad right now," I said.

"Well, she usually doesn't act up too much until we get up by the barn."

"I guess we'd better go up there then," I told her.

As we began to make our way back towards the barn, the mare remained fairly calm. But the closer we got, the more nervousness she began to show. By the time we reached the gate, it was clear that the horse was very upset. It was as if she was expecting something bad to happen to her. The woman remained calm and reassuring, speaking to the horse in low, nonthreatening tones as we made our way to the barn area. She tied the mare to one of the many hitch rails that dotted the place, and we stepped back.

The little mare immediately began to paw at the ground. She also tried to pull back lightly several times, apparently testing the strength of her lead rope. She then began to swing her rear end, first to the right, then the left, and then back again while shaking her head and blowing hard through her nose. Her eyes were wide, her nose flared, tail kinked, and muscles rigid. She acted like a horse that was getting ready to defend herself or run for her life.

"She acts like she's been beat up," I said. "I hate to ask this, but have you ever hit this horse?"

"Never," the woman replied, sadly watching her horse work herself into a lather. I couldn't help but believe her.

"Does anybody else handle her?"

"No," she said, shaking her head. "When I'm not here, she stands in pasture."

"How long has she been like this?" I asked.

"Ever since I brought her here, two months ago," she answered. "She was fine before that."

This was strange. I'd seen horses act like this before, but there was always an obvious reason for the behavior, usually mishandling or physical abuse. This one seemed to become panicked for no apparent reason. After about ten minutes of watching the mare, I began to look around for something, anything, that this horse might be seeing that could be frightening her.

Suddenly it came to me. She wasn't scared because she was being abused, but because other horses around her were. As I looked around, I saw one horse being kicked in the belly by a farrier and another being hit repeatedly with a crop. The man in the arena was still jerking on his horse, and the horse in the round pen was still being hit with a whip.

"Let's take her back to pasture," I said quietly. "I think I know what the problem is." The woman took the halter off as we passed through the pasture gate, and the mare ran all the way to the far end before turning to look back.

"I think what you have here," I started, "is a horse that's real sensitive to her surroundings. I think she's having trouble being around these other horses when they're being reprimanded." The woman looked at me like I had a tree branch growing out of the top of my head.

"I know it may sound strange," I continued, "but that's what it looks like." I went on to ask her if the type of horse handling that was going on that day by the other boarders was typical of how the horses were treated on a daily basis. She thought about it for a few minutes, then said that it was. I asked if it was common for her horse to be in the far end of the pasture whenever she'd go to catch her, and then to go back there when she was turned loose.

"It is," she answered. I told her that it was interesting that the horse remained fairly calm until we got close to the barn area and only then did she begin to panic.

"That's how she always acts," the woman admitted.

"I'm not sure," I said, "but I think all it's going to take to calm her back down is to move her to a different stable, one where there's a little less of an aggressive attitude towards the horses."

She then told me that she was taking a job in Denver and was going to be moving the mare at the end of the month anyway. She said she would take care to find such a stable before moving her. To tell you the truth, I didn't really know if that would be the answer. I'd never seen this particular problem before, so I wasn't even sure if that was causing the behavior, but it was worth a shot. I asked her to give me a call after she moved the horse and let me know if there was any change.

She said she would, and after drinking about a half-gallon of water to replenish what I'd sweated out, I climbed back into the cab of my truck, which was pushing 130 degrees. On the way home I couldn't seem to get the windows open wide enough or get the truck going fast enough to get a sufficient breeze to cool off. I was never so happy to get in the canyon that took me to the relative coolness of the mountains where I make my home.

About a month later I received a call from the woman who said she'd found a place for her horse. It was a small mom-and-pop operation with less than ten head total. The boarders were all people who were very quiet with their horses, and she said the difference in her horse was amazing. She was back to her quiet, friendly self and hadn't acted up once after the move.

Since seeing that first case of a horse being, for lack of a better term, hypersensitive to its surroundings, I suppose I have run across a couple of dozen others with varying degrees of the same symptoms. In each case, we were able to alleviate the problem almost completely by simply relocating the animal to different surroundings. It never ceases to amaze me when I see the level at which horses try to communicate when something is bothering them. For my money, understanding what they're trying to communicate is, in itself, the key to being successful at pinpointing the causes of problems that horses are having.

Unfortunately, it's usually a matter of us not understanding them, them not understanding us, and us not taking the time to try.

———————

It's been my experience that one of the most overlooked causes of problem behavior in horses is soreness—theirs, not ours. I suppose the reason it's so often overlooked is that in our minds, horses don't ever get sore. After all, they're horses. They never get sore muscles, necks, and backs. Right? Wrong. We just never take the time to look, and if we don't look, we won't find it. The horse just continues to act up, and we continue to try to correct him, often with little or no improvement. In many cases, the behavior becomes worse as the soreness intensifies.

In my first real encounter with a sore-backed horse, I found this out the hard way. The old man had given me a big paint mare that he said "bucked a little" and asked me to try to get it out of her.

"No problem," I remember saying to him as if I were Casey Tibbs.

I brought the mare out of her pen and tied her to the hitch rail just outside the tack room. I know today that the constant flinching, flicking of her tail, and the dirty glances that she gave me while I groomed her back with a brush were warning signs—signs that she was trying to tell me that it hurt when I did that. But back then, it didn't mean a thing to me, and I all but ignored them. At the most, I dismissed them as her being grumpy and spoiled.

As I threw the saddle on her back, she tried to bite me. As I cinched her up, she tried to bite me again. When I went to put my foot in the stirrup, she constantly moved away, and as I pulled myself up, she tried to cow-kick me. If I'd have known enough to look at those things as warnings from her as to what was going to happen when I climbed on, I'm sure I could have avoided the events that were about to take place.

I threw a leg over and had no sooner got my right foot in the stirrup than all hell broke loose. After about her third jump, I wished I actually was Casey Tibbs. I was fairly certain that he was the only man alive who'd be able to stay on her for eight seconds. I sure knew I wasn't going to.

It's hard to say which jump actually did it. I think it may have been the fifth. I guess it doesn't really matter. What I remember about it most is the height that I got. I recall being able to see clearly the tin roof of the hay barn as we went by.

She pitched me so high that my head was twenty feet in the air and my feet, still in the stirrups, banged together like Dorothy's in *The Wizard of Oz*. I came back down, landing unceremoniously on the saddle horn, which, by the way, can knock the wind out of a guy faster than anything else I know, not to mention the effect it has on his voice.

What I remember about it most is the height that I got.

It was shortly afterward that I recall looking up through the dust cloud, which I'd made as I hit the ground, into the face of the old man.

"Helluva wreck," he grunted. "You okay?"

"I think so," I said, after taking a quick inventory.

"Good," he said. "I'll catch your horse up." I felt honored. I had never seen the old man show that much compassion before. Usually he made you get your own horse. It must have been a good wreck.

It's hard to say how many times I came off of the mare in the following four hours, but it was enough for the old man to think that something might actually be physically wrong with her.

"Hold on," he said, as I picked myself up off the ground for the umpteenth time. "I think she's trying to tell us something."

"Yeah," I added. "She's trying to tell us that she can buck better than I can ride." That got a rare chuckle out of the old man.

"No. I think it might be something else." He walked over to where the mare was standing and pulled her saddle. He then took the heel of his hand and began pressing directly on her spine, starting at her withers and working his way towards her tail.

He had gotten only about to the middle of her back when suddenly her legs buckled from the pain he was inflicting. He had a painful look on his face as he shook his head and said, "Go ahead and put her up."

"What's wrong with her?" I asked, trying to shake the dirt out of the inside of my shirt.

"She's got a bad back," was his reply.

When I asked what could be done for it, he sadly answered, "Nothing. I'll have to haul her to the sale barn." That meant he was hauling her to slaughter.

What a waste, I remember thinking to myself. *She's such a nice-looking horse.*

To be honest, I don't know if there was something he could have done for the mare or if he simply didn't want to deal with it at the time. What I do know is that soreness plays such a big part in the causes of many problems that, to this day, it's the first thing I look for. There are several different ways that soreness can be treated—from conventional veterinary techniques, to the slightly more unconventional, such as therapeutic massage, acupressure, acupuncture, and equine chiropractic, to name a few.

While soreness is a major cause of problem behavior, it is unfortunately often difficult to detect unless you know what to look for. On the other hand, other causes are blatantly obvious, but sometimes they are still simply overlooked or ignored. I remember being present one time at a livery stable when a trail ride was returning. As the riders approached the area where the guests were to dismount, I noticed the horse directly behind the guide acting up. He was prancing and shaking his head, and as they got closer to the dismounting area, he actually broke into a trot and passed the guide. A little barn sour, I thought to myself.

"Could somebody please help the lady on Whiskey?" the guide asked in disgust. "He's been acting up the whole ride."

As one of the other wranglers made his way over to assist the woman on the horse, I noticed something peculiar about the animal's tack. The horse's saddle blanket had slipped backwards. So far, in fact, that only about six inches of the pad actually remained between the saddle and the horse. The rest of the pad was on his butt. As a result, the saddle was riding directly on the animal's withers, which were very prominent to begin with. Pulling the horse's saddle revealed a sore on his withers six inches long and an inch-and-a-half wide. The damage to his back was so extensive that he was sensitive to the touch from his neck clear back to his hip.

When the wranglers were confronted with his condition, one of them replied, "Oh, yeah, he's had a scab there all summer. I guess it's opened up again." He was completely oblivious to the fact that having an open sore might actually be causing the animal pain and, in turn, making him act barn sour. The wrangler was upset with the horse for acting up, while the horse was simply trying to get back to the barn, knowing that once there, he could get rid of the source of his pain—the rider.

I would be willing to bet that more behavioral problems are caused by ill-fitting tack than anything else except maybe straight-out physical abuse. It's certainly a very common cause. The thing about problems caused by tack is that they come on so slowly that the rider often doesn't even know anything is wrong until the horse becomes almost unmanageable.

I recall two women who had bought horses within about a week of each other and kept them at a boarding stable I happened to be training at. One was an older quarter horse gelding that was boarded in pasture. The other was a bay Morgan gelding that was kept in a box stall in the barn.

I was working in the arena on a young paint gelding when the two friends brought the horses in for the first time. Both horses were very quiet and responsive as they were put through their paces along the rail. Both owners seemed to ride quite well and appeared to be having a pretty good time. Except for an occasional stumble by the Morgan, the day passed without incident. About an hour later, I sat on the paint allowing him to rest in the middle of the arena. The two new horse owners rode up and struck up a very pleasant conversation with me.

As we were talking, I couldn't help but notice the saddles the two were using. On the quarter horse was what appeared to be a brand new show-type saddle, very fancy and shiny with a lot of doodads on it. The Morgan had on an old high-back saddle with large skirts. I also noticed that both saddles appeared to fit the riders very well, but didn't fit the horses at all. The show saddle had a very low gullet, which caused it to ride directly on the animal's withers. The other had plenty of clearance for the Morgan's withers but pinched its shoulders horribly. We soon finished our conversation, and the two went to put their horses away.

The next day I sat on the rail and watched as the two once again worked the horses in the arena. That day I noticed slight changes in both horses' attitudes and responsiveness. The Morgan was tripping more frequently than the day before due to its shoulders being constricted by the saddle. Each time he tripped, the rider would get after him by kicking him in the sides. The horse responded by lunging forward. This seemed to surprise the rider who would then pull back on the reins, which caused the horse to throw his head.

The change in the quarter horse was a little less dramatic. What I noticed about him was that each time he was asked to change from one gait to the next, he would hesitate slightly, then lay his ears back and flick his tail before making the transition.

After a week of being ridden every day, both horses were showing signs of major problems developing. The Morgan was tripping more frequently and, out of frustration, had not only continued to toss his head but was now offering to crow hop and had become more difficult to stop. The quarter horse was becoming difficult to mount and was refusing to make transitions.

By the sixth week, the Morgan had become almost uncontrollable, a disposition being helped along by the four pounds of sweet feed, a source of pure energy, he was getting every day while standing in his stall. The quarter horse, in contrast, would make every effort not to allow his rider on. Once the rider was on, he would simply refuse to move. He'd stand in one place while the rider, who had taken to wearing spurs and carrying a crop, would flail away mercilessly in an attempt to get some movement, any movement out of him. Within three months' time, both horses, because of the major problems they had developed, went up for sale.

Now, some people might say, "If you saw the problems developing, why didn't you say something or try to help?" The answer to that is simple. The owners didn't ask. Like the old man said, you can't help somebody who doesn't want to be helped, especially when it comes to them and their horses.

There's no crime in having a horse develop a training problem. It happens every day to horses all over the world. And to tell the truth, there are as many problem causes as there are horses and horse owners. The ones I've described are simply the most common. If it happens to you, it certainly doesn't mean that you're automatically deemed the Gomer Pyle of the horse industry. It simply means that you've run into a little trouble. If you can't get yourself out of it, try looking for help from somebody who knows what they're doing, not from someone who just thinks they know what they're doing. That's how you got yourself in trouble to begin with. You need someone with extensive experience in the specific problem you're having.

Like I said, it's no crime to have your horse develop a problem. The crime comes when you allow it to continue, or worse, have to sell the animal to someone who can take advantage of the situation, and in turn, make money from your mistakes.

If there's one thing I have come to understand over the years, it's that every problem horses develop, and I mean every problem, is man-made. Plain and simple. They certainly haven't asked to be domesticated by us, so how can we possibly blame them when things go wrong? It's like driving your car into a tree, then blaming the tree because it was in your way. If we're going to solve the many problems that horses develop, we first have to find the source, and all it takes to do that is a mirror.

NOTES FOR PROBLEM CAUSES

I think most trainers at one time or another get to working with a horse whose problem behavior seems pretty straightforward and relatively easy to work through at first, only to find no matter how much work they put into the horse, the training doesn't seem to stick. Several years before writing this book, I had had a string of horses just like that, and it was those horses that got me trying to figure out where the problems were coming from instead of just how to fix them.

In this chapter I mentioned what, to me at the time, were relatively obvious causes of problem behavior and ones I had been studying pretty closely in the years preceding the book. In reading the chapter now, I can see how many more potential causes for unwanted behavior I had actually left out, such as the horse having bad teeth, unbalanced feet/poor shoeing or trimming, the effects certain feeds have on horses, and bad saddle fit—just to name a few.

When this book originally came out, I was at the very beginning of what would ultimately turn into a nearly thirty-year quest to learn more about horse physiology, psychology, anatomy, joint function, vision, hoof care, feed, tooth care and herd structure. While my main goal in writing this chapter was to get people to start thinking about the causes of their horse's unwanted behavior, instead of just trying to fix it, I realize now that I just didn't have enough information at the time to include more things to look for.

Still, it is one of the chapters I look back on and think, *If I only knew then what I know now* . . .

Unfixable problems

I knocked on the back door of the old farm house, and a dog began to bark from inside. As a rule, it's not too difficult to judge a dog's size by the sound its feet make when they hit the floor as it runs to the door. If the sound is a fast, high-pitched click as it runs across the kitchen linoleum, chances are it's a small or medium-size dog. If, on the other hand, you hear several thuds as the dog crosses the carpet in the living room, then a clacking sound as it comes across the linoleum, you've probably got a pretty big one heading your way.

That was the case with this dog. The one other thing that told me this dog was going to be big was the way the windows of the house shook every time it put a foot down. From the inside of the house, I heard a woman's voice say, "Clancy. Quiet! Sit down and behave yourself."

The barking stopped, and I could hear what appeared to be a swishing sound. Apparently the dog was now sweeping the floor with its tail as it sat by the woman's side awaiting the opening of the door.

"Hi," I said, introducing myself when the door finally opened. "I believe your husband wanted me to look at a horse he's having trouble with."

"Oh, you're the horse trainer," the woman said, smiling. "John had to go get a part for the mower. He should be home any time though."

"No problem," I told her. "I can wait." Sitting on the floor next to her was a monster of a dog, half golden lab and half Welsh pony, I think.

"Can I interest you in something to drink while you wait?"

I stood for a moment looking at Dogzilla, when she smiled and said, "Clancy doesn't bite. Mostly he's just big."

"Well, actually," I replied politely, "I'd rather have a look at the horse, if that'd be all right."

"Oh, sure," she smiled. "He should be in the corral. If he's not there, he's probably in the barn." She paused for a moment, then said, "Maybe I should go with you. He doesn't like strangers much."

As the three of us (the woman, Clancy, and myself) made our way towards the corral, her husband, John, pulled into the driveway. Clancy immediately turned and ran over to him, looking like a moose running through a swamp. I was hoping that in his enthusiasm the dog wouldn't jump on John. If he did, it would mean certain death for the man. Luckily, the dog stopped short of where John was and quietly sat down. John walked over, gave the dog a brief pat on the head, and continued towards us with Clancy following close behind.

With introductions out of the way and the woman and Clancy heading back to the house, John began to explain the history of the horse I'd come to see. He had acquired the two-year-old only a few months earlier as a stallion. The horse had been running in a 170-acre pasture out on the plains with thirty or forty other horses until the past winter. That winter on the plains had been particularly harsh, and the herd's owner had left the horses to fend for themselves. As a result, nearly half the herd literally starved to death, and the rest, including this horse, had been well on their way.

By the time the surviving horses were reported and subsequently confiscated by state officials, most were so poor that they literally had to be hand-lifted into trailers for relocation and rehabilitation. Three more horses died upon arriving at the rehab center, but luckily this one survived. John then acquired the horse, a sorrel mustang-looking thing, from an adoption center while it was still pretty thin and weak.

As the horse gained weight and got his strength back, John began to notice strange behavior. Among other things, the horse would sometimes panic for no apparent reason, often while standing alone in pasture. Also, the only way he could be caught was to lure him into the barn with food and then close the door behind him. Catching him in the corral or adjacent ten-acre pasture was impossible. Once caught, he was extremely unpredictable. One day he would be as quiet as a church mouse. The next, he'd be rearing, striking, biting, and kicking.

John had had the horse gelded hoping that would settle him down, but apparently it hadn't. To compound the problems, the horse's feet were in terrible shape and needed immediate attention. Three separate farriers had been called in to try to fix his feet. One had to drug the horse; the other two had to restrain him by scotch-hobbling him. Still, one farrier was injured when the horse kicked him in the knee. John had come to the conclusion that, even though he had owned horses all his life, he was in over his head with this one and needed help.

"Well," I said, "let's have a look at him."

A quick look in the corral told us he wasn't there, and the closed gate to the pasture meant he was in the barn. John slowly opened the large sliding door to the barn to show the horse sleeping in the cool darkness of his 10-by-14-foot box stall. We quietly approached and stood outside the stall's heavy wooden gate. The horse looked at us and snorted. After only a few seconds, he began to inch his way closer, stopping far enough away that it took every inch of his outstretched neck to get his nose close enough to get a good whiff of us.

John and I stood very still and quiet so as not to frighten him unnecessarily. Suddenly, and without warning, the horse squealed, spun on his back end, and stampeded out the door into the corral. He crossed the forty-foot corral in no time flat and jumped the five-foot fence into the adjacent pasture. In less time than it takes for a drunkard to fall down a flight of steps, he was at the far end of the pasture snorting, pawing, and shaking his head.

"Oh, yeah," John said, as we stood looking at each other. "He jumps fences, too."

I wanted to get a better look at the horse, so we slowly made our way into the pasture. He responded by running the entire ten-acre fence line at full speed. We stood in the middle of the pasture while the horse ran frantically around us. As we stood watching the horse's apparent lack of self control, John began to relate more stories of his unexplainable behavior. He talked of how the horse would act extremely depressed for two or three days, sometimes even go off his feed. Then suddenly he would be terribly aggressive, trying to attack anything or anybody passing near the fence. Once he even attacked the side of the barn, first trying to bite it, then kicking it with his hind feet. He had done the same with the wooden corral fence.

"Let me ask you this," I said, as the horse stopped near the fence and began throwing what I can only call a temper tantrum. "How attached to this horse are you?"

"Why?" he asked. "Do you think he's too far gone?"

"Maybe," I told him. "He's definitely got some major problems."

I went on to explain that nearly all "problem horses," no matter how bad they are, generally fall into certain boundaries of normal horse behavior. That is, behavior that is normal to the horse as a species, even if the behavior is at the extreme edge of being normal. This horse appeared to be past that point. He was showing behavior that no horse in its right mind would exhibit.

"In other words," I said, pointing to my head, "I think he's got something wrong upstairs."

"What would cause that?" he asked, as we began to make our way back to the barn.

"Well, from what you've told me and from what we're seeing here, my guess is he's inbred."

"That makes sense," he said. "A bunch of the horses in that herd were stallions." He paused for a moment as if he were in thought. "Is there anything that can be done for him?"

"Unfortunately," I started, "in all of the cases that I've seen like this, there isn't much hope of making them right." I went on to explain that often close inbreeding does such extensive damage to the animal's brain that, mentally, it simply can't function properly. As a result, its thought processes are distorted, and it ends up doing things that are dangerous not only to itself, but to everything and everybody around it.

I had no sooner finished saying that when the horse, as if to put an exclamation point to the statement, charged us. We were within about ten feet of the corral fence and wasted no time getting up and over it on our way to the safety of the barn. We had only gotten about half way across the corral when we heard a sickening crashing behind us.

I turned around in time to see the horse breaking through the top three rails of the four-rail fence that separated us. He tripped on the remaining bottom rail and landed in the most hideous position on the right side of his face, flipping over in such a way that I was sure he'd broken his neck. Much to my surprise, however, he was quickly back on his feet, quietly standing as if to say, "Great trick, huh? For my next one I'm going to crash through the barn."

"Maybe I should just put him down," John said, as we both stood shaking our heads at what had just transpired. "Is that what you would do?"

"That has to be your decision," I told him. "The one thing I will say is this, though. I don't believe he'll ever make a good horse for you, no matter how much training you put into him."

As I left John's place and headed back down the gravel road I'd come in on, I couldn't help but think of the similarities between this horse and another I'd worked with a couple of years earlier, a gray mare named Dusty that had been given to me by a woman who simply couldn't handle her. The one stipulation that she made when she gave me the horse was that I try to get her trained. What I soon came to find out was that Dusty had some problems that were bigger than both of us.

She had days when she was completely unpredictable, even aggressive, followed by days when she'd be so quiet that you weren't sure she was even the same horse. I remember one day in particular. I had just caught her and was leading her down to the barn when suddenly she just blew the cork. She pulled away from me by rearing and violently shaking her head. After getting away, she went only a few feet and began spinning and bucking in place. After a short time, she stopped and looked at me. The look of terror that was on her face slowly dissipated into one I can only call helplessness.

A couple of days later she did the same thing; only this time at the end of the tantrum, she ran directly into the side of the nearby barn, scraping her head and shoulder before stopping. To this day, it's hard to explain the feeling I got when she looked at me. I swear that she was saying, "Can you please help me?" That had made such an impression on me that I recall telling a friend of mine, Susie Hiede, that I felt like the mare was trying to tell me something.

Less than a week later, while grazing with one other horse in a five-acre pasture, the mare suddenly panicked for no apparent reason. A lady, who happened to be nearby when the incident occurred, said the horse was grazing peacefully when all of a sudden she turned and began running as fast as she could. When she came upon the four-strand barbed wire fence that enclosed the pasture, she never slowed a beat and hit it at full speed.

By the time I got to her, she was standing quietly about a quarter mile away, being tended to by Susie. The injuries she sustained when she went through the fence were so severe that there was no question that she'd have to be put down. I immediately went to the truck and returned with my rifle. As I approached, she nickered as if to say, "There . . . that's what I've been trying to tell you all along. Finally, now you understand."

Certainly there is no way to know for sure if, in fact, that horse had been trying to "talk" to me. But I can't help but think what a tragedy it would be if she were, and I didn't

We heard a sickening crashing behind us.

make the effort to listen. After all, in my opinion, the whole point of being a horse trainer or a horse owner, for that matter, is to be able to communicate what we need from the horse in a way it can understand. What good is that, if we aren't willing to pay attention when the horse tries to communicate back?

Now, as I drove away from John's place, I was getting the same feeling from his horse that I'd gotten from Dusty, a feeling that he was using his abnormal behavior as a cry for help.

The problem with this theory is just that. It's only a theory. Even less, it's a feeling. It's difficult for me to make a decision concerning a horse's future, or lack thereof, on a feeling. I might be able to look at a horse like John's and justify his behavior as if he is trying to say, "Hey, I don't want to live like this anymore." But I simply can't bring myself to tell that to the owner.

So, in John's case, I simply explained what I felt was causing the problem and told him what kind of life a horse like that would likely have. In turn, this leaves the decision for the horse's future where it should be, in the hands of the owner. There are other times, however, when I do feel qualified to intervene and in turn suggest that perhaps a certain horse and owner are not meant for each other.

There was a time in my life when I truly felt that any problem could be overcome if you could just come up with the proper training technique. In many ways, I still feel that way. Unfortunately, as is often the case, youthful enthusiasm has been tempered by the harsh realities of experience, and idealism has been replaced by the hard, cold facts of life in the horse business.

In other words, in the real world, trying to save every single horse with a major problem simply isn't feasible, financially or logistically, for most horse owners, not to mention the mental strain it often puts on them or the serious injury or property damage the horse may cause in the meantime.

When I see these types of circumstances, I can't help but suggest that the horse's owner cut his or her losses by getting rid of the animal and finding one he or she can get along with. I know that may sound somewhat cruel to the horse, but as I see it, owning horses should be a give-and-take proposition between horse and owner. If all attempts to accomplish that have failed or when there is such a complete breakdown of trust that the animal is no longer safe to own, then I see no reason for it to continue to be around. What I am talking about here are serious, deep-rooted mental problems that make an animal completely unsafe, not minor training problems that can be overcome in thirty, sixty, or even ninety days.

I was called in once to do some training at a guest ranch where they raised their own stock for the dude string. Obviously this meant doing the breeding, foaling, and training right there on the place. The reason I'd been called was that the fellow who had been doing the training had taken another job and was leaving a half dozen two- and three-year-olds unbroke. They wanted them at least green broke so that wranglers could guide off them when the season started, four months later. I was assured by the ranch owner that none of the colts had any problems and were all very quiet.

Now, I realized long ago that when some people discuss how good their unbroke horse's behavior is, that I should probably roll up my pant legs and watch where I step. So, for the life of me, I don't know why I was surprised to find what I did on my first day at the ranch. There were six horses all right. But to say they didn't have any problems was like saying a nine-pound sparrow isn't fat. All six were in a 40-by-40-foot corral. There were two mares and four geldings, and all were what I can only describe as basket cases.

I spent the first two days teaching them all how to stand still long enough for me to approach them with a halter in my hand. Of the four that would allow me to approach and subsequently halter them, only two knew how to lead. Of those two, only one would lead through the gate and away from the others. It took another week to be able to do the same thing with the other three.

It didn't take long to figure out that much of the trouble the colts seemed to be having stemmed from previous mishandling. All six appeared to have several rope burns on their lower legs, and certain surroundings, such as the round pen, terrified them. The sight of a longe whip or lead rope would often send them all stampeding off into an uncontrollable frenzy, and any type of sudden movement on my part warranted defensive behavior on theirs.

Even so, four of the six responded to training and settled down relatively quickly, all within two to six weeks. It soon became apparent that the remaining two had problems that were a little more severe. One was a black gelding, the other a bay, and neither was interested in trying to be a horse. Both were very explosive and unpredictable, which made doing the simplest of tasks, such as putting a halter on or even approaching them, extremely dangerous.

At one point, while slowly buckling the black's halter in place, he suddenly blew, catching the ring finger of my right hand between his head and the halter as he went. The telltale snapping sound quickly told me that the finger was no longer intact, and after freeing it from the halter, my suspicion about breaking it was confirmed.

It was a nasty break between the first and second knuckle that caused the end of the finger to go off at an angle that was never intended. Knowing that the nerves around a fracture are temporarily in shock, I quickly grabbed the end of the finger and jerked it back in place. In the meantime, the black was stampeding around the corral wearing the halter with the lead rope dragging between his legs. It took nearly thirty minutes before he finally decided to stop and another thirty before I was able to catch him and remove the halter.

It soon became apparent that the one thing that horse did best was explode. He would do it any time, any place, and for reasons known only to him. He was good at it, too. He could blow with more enthusiasm than any horse I had ever seen and was so unpredictable he was actually becoming predictable. You knew it was going to happen; you just didn't know exactly when.

The bay's behavior was very similar. The biggest difference was that when he'd blow, he didn't care who or what was in front of him. It didn't matter. He'd either run through or over whatever or whoever was in his way.

Neither horse seemed to be able to retain any of the training information I was trying to pass along. Even the simplest things needed to be shown to them over and over again. While the other four were not only being ridden but also learning difficult maneuvers like side passing, those two were still learning to be caught and accept the halter.

Sixty days of quiet handling didn't appear to help the bay at all. In fact, he suddenly had become unapproachable and often violent. The decision was made to discontinue his training and sell him at auction. Sixty days after that, the same decision was made with the black.

A check into the breeding records of both horses showed that, due to accidental breedings in both of the dams' immediate family trees, both colts had received a tremendous amount of genetic imbalance. The result was a couple of horses that were no good to themselves or anybody else.

Inbreeding isn't the only thing that will cause strange behavior in horses, though. I was called out to a woman's home to see a horse she had recently brought home from winter pasture. The horse, she said, was acting "very weird" and not at all like himself. When I arrived at the place, the woman took me in the barn and showed me a very thin, fifteen-hand Morgan. The horse was standing quietly in a box stall and, other than his emaciated state, he looked quite normal.

The woman must have noticed the concern on my face as I gazed upon the horse's protruding ribs and hip bones. She quickly began to explain that she had left the horse in a friend's fairly large pasture in the foothills for the winter. She had been traveling during that time and had assurances from the friend that the horse would be well cared for, but obviously it hadn't been. When she arrived at the end of May to pick the horse up, this

He suddenly blew, catching the ring finger of my right hand.

emaciated horse was what she'd found. Not only was the horse terribly thin, he wasn't acting like himself either.

"Let me show you what I'm talking about," she said, snapping a lead rope to the halter that was already on the horse's head and leading him outside.

As soon as the horse got outside, his demeanor changed. He was suddenly very spooky, so much so that he was literally afraid of his own shadow, jumping at the sight of it four or five times in a matter of about thirty seconds. The woman slowly led him around the corral and his behavior became more and more peculiar. He snorted at "ghosts," spooked at imaginary snakes, and stepped over logs that weren't there.

A sudden stiff breeze picked up, catching the horse's tail and whipping the end of it around so that it hit him on the right rear leg. He jumped like somebody hit him in the butt with a hot shot, nearly running over the woman. The longer he stood in the corral, the more panicked he became. He began to shake nervously and spin around in an attempt to see in every direction at the same time.

"Now, watch this," the woman said, leading him back into the barn.

As he reached his box stall, he relaxed immediately. Except for an occasional glance backward, out the barn door, there was no sign of the terrified animal we had seen only seconds earlier.

"Isn't that weird?" she said, unsnapping the lead rope from the halter. "What can be causing that and how can I fix it?"

"Well," I said sadly, "I don't believe I can help you. I think what you need here is a vet."

"You think he's sick?" she asked in surprise.

"I'm not sure," I told her, "but he kind of acts like he's been locoed."

"What's that?" she asked.

"Locoweed," I replied. "It's a plant that's toxic to horses. As a rule, they won't even touch it unless they're starving to death."

I went on to explain that locoweed grows in semi-arid regions like the foothills where this horse wintered and is usually the first thing that comes up in the spring. If there was no feed left on the pasture, he probably ate the first green plant he saw growing. "And if it was locoweed," I told her, "this horse is in trouble."

"Oh, God." There was a sense of urgency in her voice. "What can we do for him?"

"Now hold on," I said, trying to calm her. "I'm not absolutely sure that locoweed is the problem here. That's why you should get ahold of your vet. There's always a possibility that it's something else."

"Yeah, but what if locoweed is the problem?" she replied. "Then what?"

I stood quiet for a long time, trying to find the right words to answer her question.

"You see," I started, "the problem with locoweed is that before it does any damage, horses have to eat a whole lot of it. Something like ninety percent of their body weight in about thirty days time." I could see the concern start to cross her face.

"Once they eat that much," I continued, "the toxins begin to eat away at the brain." I paused for a minute, not wanting to say the rest. "The damage is usually irreversible."

"Usually?" she asked, with a glimmer of hope in her voice.

"Well," I felt myself stammering. "Actually, it's always irreversible."

She was about to say something more when I broke in. "But before you get yourself worked up," I pointed out, "call your vet. He'll be able to tell you for sure what's going on here. Like I said, I'm not absolutely sure locoweed is your problem."

I probably would never have known what became of that horse had I not happened to run into the woman at the National Western Stock Show in Denver seven months later. Unfortunately, as it turned out, I'd been correct in my assumption. The woman said that she'd made an effort to tend to the horse, but under her vet's advice, she decided to have him put to sleep after only a couple of months.

While the result of inbreeding and this type of toxic poisoning in horses is usually tragic, the truth of the matter is, the circumstances that caused them to occur are often accidental or, at most, done out of ignorance as to what the consequences to the horse may be. So, in a way, I guess the people who cause these types of problems can be forgiven. However, I have seen major behavior problems similar to those of inbred and poisoned horses for which there are no excuses for the cause—abuse.

I have seen horses that, among other things, had been snubbed to posts and beaten with ball bats, 2 × 4s, and pitch forks. Others have been flogged with chains and heavy leather straps, and still others that were tortured with hot shots and boards with nails in them. In one case, I even saw a horse that had barbed wire wrapped around his middle. The wire was attached to a long rope, and each time the horse did something wrong, his owner would jerk on the rope.

As much mental and physical damage as these things caused those horses, there was one horse whose abuse was so lengthy and severe that, to this day, I have seen none worse. He is also the one horse that has taught me more about dealing with the mind of an abused horse than any other. His name was Domino.

When I first met Domino, he was fourteen years old. A very flashy and well-built appaloosa gelding, he had been purchased by a couple of my friends who wanted to use him as a trail horse. Domino's problems surfaced almost immediately, and I was called in to see if I could help him overcome them.

Unfortunately, it didn't take long to see that Domino's problems were deep rooted and as bad as they come. He had a tremendous fear of anything that walked on two legs and, as a result, was very difficult to catch, no matter what size enclosure he was in. In a large enclosure, he'd run away. In a small one, he'd stand with his head in a corner and shake terribly. If you tried to approach, he'd swing his butt directly at you, more as an evasive action than a threat. He was extremely headshy and any attempt to touch him in any way would cause him to panic.

Trying to saddle or bridle him was nearly impossible and just the sight of a saddle blanket would send him into the next county. In fact, we thought about changing his name to Wyoming, because one wrong move on our part, and that's where we'd have to go to get him.

A lengthy check into his background turned up that his abuse began as early as when he was a two-year-old and continued until he was purchased by his current owners, Pat and Bob. It didn't take long to figure out that getting through to him was not going to be easy nor was it going to happen overnight.

It took three weeks to get his trust up enough to where he was catchable. He still wasn't necessarily easy to catch, but he was better than he had been. It was months before he ceased being headshy and still more months before he was accepting the saddle. During the year or so that I was able to work with him, he had gained an uneasy trust in Pat, Bob, and myself, mostly because we were the ones handling him. Trusting strangers was still out of the question.

Unfortunately, his years of abuse not only caused him damage mentally, but physically as well. He had a chronic sore neck, shoulder, and ribs, and there was deterioration in the muscles of his hind quarters that caused him to be short-strided in the right rear.

The year of slow, consistent work with Domino paid off in vast improvements on his part. And although we were still unable to ride him, he had gained enough trust in us that he would quietly accept just about anything we asked of him. However, about a year after we'd started working with him, we found that, because of damage to his ribs, cinching him up caused him unbearable pain. The decision was made to cease his training until the problem could be fixed and he had ample time to heal.

About a month after his training stopped, I went to the stable where he was being boarded. As I drove in, I saw him tied to a rail with Pat quietly grooming him. I walked over and struck up a conversation with her as she continued brushing. As we were talking, I slowly brought my hand up to stroke Domino on the shoulder as I'd done thousands of times over the past year. Sadly, he responded by fearfully stepping away from my hand, as if he had never seen me before and I posed a threat.

"Domino," Pat said, as if comforting a frightened child. "It's just Mark."

"That's okay," I told her. "I guess he hasn't seen me in a while."

The sad part about what happened to Domino is the fact that he will probably never be right again. He will always be leery of strangers and, in a sense, be waiting for the other shoe to drop. Had it not been for people like Pat and Bob taking him in, I'm fairly certain that he'd be dead by now—just one more horse gone to slaughter because nobody could get along with him.

The unfortunate thing is that Domino isn't alone. There are thousands of horses out there just like him, horses that are abused from the time they hit the ground until the day they die. Those horses usually end up with such severe mental problems that if they're lucky enough to end up in the hands of somebody who can help them, they're usually too far gone to save.

Now I'm certainly not trying to sound like Mr. Gloom-and-Doom here. The truth of the matter is, if a horse's problems aren't mental to start with, there is a better-than-average chance of them being fixed. You simply need to know the animal's limitations, both physical and mental, and be able to work within those boundaries.

It has been my experience that, if you can learn how to do that, and you can catch the horse before too much damage is done, anything is possible. At the very least, you could be saving him from a one-way trip to the slaughter house. At the very most, you could have a lifelong friend and trusted companion.

NOTES FOR UNFIXABLE PROBLEMS

A few years after this book originally came out, I ran across a horse that seemed to fit into the "unfixable problem" category. Every effort had been made to make sure the horse was physically comfortable including chiropractic care, acupuncture treatments, having its teeth done by a reputable equine dentist, top-notch foot care, proper diet, and even a well-fitting saddle. Still, it seemed any training the horse was offered simply didn't go in and I was beginning to think the little horse might be a lost cause. I was about two months into working with the gelding when I happened to read an article in a magazine about ulcers in horses and how they can affect the horses behavior and attitude.

A quick check with a vet, some stomach medication, and just like that, the horse's potentially "unfixable problem" behavior was gone. It was a reminder to me that while the issues I spoke about in this particular chapter are very real and do occur, it is still extremely important to exhaust all resources before giving up on a horse who seems beyond help . . . something I always wished I had stressed more when originally writing the chapter.

Part Two
Ground Problems

A gasp of amazement went up from the crowd at the ease at which he was able to approach the previously unapproachable horse. An even bigger gasp went up as he turned to make his way back to the middle of the pen, and the horse wearily followed as if it were a lost puppy following a little boy to a new home.

"Isn't that amazing?" I overheard one woman say to her friend sitting next to me.

Amazing, I thought to myself, *I guess that's one way to describe it, although parlor trick might be a little more accurate description.* Most of the people who were attending that day as spectators appeared to be your average backyard horse owners. That is, folks who don't make a living with horses, but rather own them for pleasure riding and nothing more. I'm sure that in their eyes what they had just witnessed was indeed nothing short of magical. What's more, to hear the trainer talk, they too could perform the magic, if only they bought his lead rope, because truly therein lies the magic.

Well, the truth of the matter is, there was no magic in what he did, and there is no need for a specially designed lead rope to catch a hard-to-catch horse. All it really takes is a little understanding, know-how, and timing. Of course, saying that won't sell many lead ropes, but then again, selling lead ropes isn't a concern of mine.

I must admit, though, I know how the spectators at the clinic must have felt that day. Seeing the ease with which a trainer is able to accomplish something that, to them, is extremely difficult, if not impossible, would seem like a revelation. I remember watching for the first time as the old man went out and caught a horse that nobody else could get near. I thought it was the Second Coming. The difference was he didn't try to pass it off as that. Instead he took the time to explain that what he was doing was allowing the horse to feel comfortable enough to want to be caught.

What the trainer did in his demonstration was simply a variation on that idea. The difference was that instead of allowing the horse the time to become comfortable with the idea of being caught, it appeared that he made the horse so tired that it had no alternative. He then tried to pass it off as him communicating what he wanted to the horse and the horse understanding.

Unfortunately, the problem I saw was that many of the people left the clinic that day thinking that all they'd need to fix their hard-to-catch horse was the magic lead rope and enough room to get the horse tuckered out.

The truth is, running the horse around until it gets tired will probably work the first time or two. After that, what they will have is a horse that thinks that every time people come near, they want the horse to run away. So, instead of fixing the problem, they will actually make it worse. All they will have to show for their trouble is a new lead rope with the magic worn off and a horse that heads for the tall timber every time they come around.

The reason I know this is that over the years I have either seen or used just about every horse-catching trick there is, from hiding a halter behind my back as I approached, to shaking a grain bucket and using a lariat to rope the horse. The one thing I have come to understand during that time is that no trick in the world is as good as simply teaching the horse how to be caught to begin with. The thing is, most people don't know how to do that, so they rely on the "tricks," usually a bucket full of grain or herding the animal into a small enclosure where they can corner it.

Now I'm not trying to say that there is anything wrong with people tricking their horses into being caught. In fact, it's usually a pretty good way for both horse and owner to get a little extra exercise. What I will say is this—if people used half the energy and brain power that it takes to develop and then implement these tricks on actually teaching the horse how to be caught, they would never have another hard-to-catch horse as long as they lived.

One of the first horses I tried to catch was a chubby little paint gelding. For years he'd been the pet of a little girl who'd now grown into a teenager and had discovered boys. Subsequently, the horse did nothing but stand around in a 30-by-50-foot pen in the family's backyard.

I'd been contacted by the girl's father, who had decided to sell the little horse, to come out and ride it for a couple of weeks and get a few of the kinks out. Hopefully, he thought, if the horse rode halfway decent, he might be able to get a little better price for it and, in turn, help make up for its staggering feed bill.

I asked the man, upon arriving at the house, if the horse had any quirks I should be concerned with before I got started.

"Well," he said, looking over the corral fence at the plump little horse standing impatiently by his feed trough. "He's a little spoiled and hard to catch."

"Will he come to grain?" I asked, knowing full well that any horse of his size would likely go anywhere as long as food was involved.

"He will," the man replied, "but as soon as he sees a halter, he's gone."

With that bit of good news, I went into the nearby two-stall garage where the horse's feed was kept and dug a coffee can full of grain out of the open sack sitting on the floor. I also grabbed the halter off the hook, above which proudly hung a gold plaque with the name "Prince" emblazoned on it.

As I entered the corral, I discreetly hid the halter behind my back in my right hand and shook the can of grain with my left. Prince, who had since made his way over to the water trough, snapped his head to attention. Still licking his lips, he let out a low nicker as if to say, "Lunch is served." It was apparent that he'd forgotten all about the water in his mouth, because as he licked his lips, it spewed out on the ground at his feet.

He wasted no time covering the thirty or so feet between us, zeroing in on the coffee can like he was a guided missile. In his haste to get to the grain, he had completely dismissed the fact that I was attached to the can. He jammed his nose deep into the feed and at the same time shoved me with his shoulder.

He munched greedily on the grain without even taking his nose out of the can. He then jammed it back down to get an even bigger mouthful. The force with which he pushed his head into the can dislodged it from my hand and spilled the grain, can and all, in a pile on the ground. His head went to it like metal to a magnet.

I figured, seeing's how he appeared to be occupied, this would be a good time to put his halter on. I slowly began to bring the halter from behind my back. It was no sooner within his eyesight than he began to inch away, head still on the ground. As I brought the lead rope near his shoulder in an attempt to slide it over his neck, he suddenly squealed and bolted.

With his head and tail held high, he defiantly jogged away. Now I'm sure he was trying to make himself look like the proud and dignified horse that he'd always wanted to be, but unfortunately he could only manage looking like a rusted Volkswagen rolling downhill. He reached the end of the corral, then turned as if he'd forgotten something. You could read the expression on his face—*Oh, yeah, I need a drink.* With that he slowly made his way back to the water tank.

I could see right away that trying to trick this horse into being caught wasn't going to work. I knew if I was going to catch him at all, he was going to have to agree to it. That was the rub—getting him to agree.

Knowing now that hiding the halter was of no use, I began to approach him with it in plain view. I didn't even get within ten feet of him before he turned and ran off. He went less than twenty feet, then fell back into a lazy walk. I followed. I tried to keep my walk at a fairly brisk pace so as to close ground on him as he moved away, but that was of no use. Each time I closed the gap to within about ten feet, he would jog ahead, increasing the distance between us to twenty.

It was very clear that he was prepared to play this little game of keep-away for as long as I wanted to feel like a fool, which wasn't long. I decided that if he was going to keep moving away from me, the least I could do was to dictate the pace at which he was moving. After I again closed the gap to within ten feet, he began his slow jog to increase the gap. This time, however, as he began to jog, I took the end of the lead rope and quickly slapped it three or four times on the ground. The horse jumped like he'd been bit by a snake and took off running. I followed at a walk swinging the lead rope.

He ran three very fast laps around the corral, which appeared to take every ounce of energy he had, before sliding to a stop. As soon as he stopped, I did, too. I also stopped swinging the lead rope. What I was trying to show him was that as long as he was moving away from me, he was going to have to work. If he stood still, which is what I wanted, he could rest.

I let him stand quietly for a few minutes before slowly trying to approach again. I hadn't even taken three steps when he bolted and ran off. This time I stood in the middle of the corral swinging the rope, and he ran in a circle around me. He made about ten laps before stopping and turning to look at me. Again, I stopped what I was doing. I also stepped backwards to show him that if he stopped and stood still, I would move farther away, taking even more pressure off him. I made sure to stand still for at least two minutes to see what, if any, reaction he would have to me.

He had none. In fact, towards the end of the two minutes, he actually began to lose interest and started to walk away. As he did, I began to follow, this time without swinging the rope. He turned his head to watch me follow him. As he did, I stopped. I was hoping that I could at least show him that even if he looked at me I'd try to take the pressure off.

It didn't work. He simply took the opportunity to get farther away, so I resumed swinging the rope and he resumed running. This went on for about five minutes before I saw a sudden and unexpected change in him. While backing away to reward him for his most recent stop, he suddenly turned and began to walk towards me. It was obvious that he was tired, but he also appeared to have a look of resignation about him. His tail no longer had the happy-go-lucky kink in it. There was no spring in his step, and his head was peanut-rolling low. Nevertheless, as long as he continued to approach, I continued to back away.

We had gone about twenty feet before I decided to stop. He, however, continued to approach and didn't stop until he was standing inches from my chest. I wanted to pet him at this point, but remembered something that the old man had told me. He said that you always want to reward horses for doing the right thing, but with a spoiled horse, it doesn't hurt to let him work a little harder for the reward.

I stood there with the horse for only a few seconds before stepping to one side and slowly walking towards his back end. The horse, as if drawn by some overwhelming force, turned and followed. For the next ten minutes, the two of us walked together all over the inside of that corral. I would change direction at will, and he would follow as if he were lost and I was his only hope of finding his way.

I stopped and finally petted him on his neck, shoulders, and face before gently sliding the halter over his nose and buckling it in place. I led him only a few feet, slipped the halter off, and left the corral. While I spoke with his owner, he stood patiently by the gate as if waiting for permission to go do something else.

"Aren't you going to ride him?" the man asked.

"Well," I said, looking back at the still stationary horse, "I don't think so."

"That is what I'm paying you for," he pointed out.

"Yes sir," I replied, "but I think that part of the reason this horse has become hard to catch to begin with is that every time he's been caught in the past, he's been worked. I'd like him to know that just because I've caught him doesn't mean I'm going to work him."

"That's ridiculous," the man said, this time with a hint of agitation in his voice. "He doesn't want to be caught because he's spoiled. What he needs is to be ridden, and if you won't do it, I'll find someone who will."

"I didn't say I wasn't going to ride him," I told him. "I will. I'd just like a couple of days to work through this catching thing first."

That day holds special meaning for me for a couple of reasons. The first is that I was able to catch a horse that didn't want to be caught using a technique that didn't involve "tricking" him. The second is that it was the first time I turned down a training job because the owner wanted me to do something that I didn't feel was right for the horse. Over the years, I've had to do both of these things more times than I care to remember.

Another very positive thing came out of that day. The owner of the paint mentioned to some of his friends the apparent ease with which I had caught his horse. Of course, he was fitting it in while he was telling them that I refused to ride the horse, but it didn't matter. Suddenly I was getting calls from his buddies who were having trouble catching their horses, asking if I could help them.

The next six horses that I went to catch were all very similar to the chubby little paint—fat and spoiled, and yes, hard to catch. Luckily, though, by using the exact same technique, I was able to get each of them caught in forty-five minutes or less, caught to the point where they would quietly follow me without even wearing a halter.

Well, needless to say, I was feeling pretty confident in my horsemanship abilities when it came to catching hard-to-catch horses. That is, until I got to my seventh hard-to-catch horse. It was a gray Arab gelding. His owner, a tall, thin woman, showed me the way over to his pen, situated at the end of an old, run-down barn. It was late afternoon in the early fall, and the sun was just getting ready to set. This seemed to suck all the heat out of the day, and as we stood in the cool fall air, she began to tell me about the horse.

He was ten years old and very high strung. She had owned him for a very short time and had yet to be able to ride him because he was impossible to catch. She also told me some other things about him, but not thinking that they'd be relevant to what I was about to do, I began to daydream and didn't hear a word she said.

I remember feeling very smug and sure of myself as I entered the corral, halter and lead rope at the ready. The horse bolted for the other end of the corral and slid to a stop with his head sticking out nervously over the top rail of the five-and-a-half-foot wooden rail fence. Strange, I thought to myself, none of the others ran like that. Of course, what I was about to find out was there was nothing about this horse that would be like the others.

I began to approach the gelding, walking towards his butt and swinging the lead rope, just like I had with all the others. The closer I got, the more panicked he became. He began to jig furiously in place and, with his head still over the fence, move his body from side to side.

I was still more than fifteen feet away when he suddenly tried in vain to jump the fence. Luckily, he was too close to the fence to get over it, but he did manage to get his left front leg caught between the top and second rail, which sent him into an even more severe panic. I stopped my advance and helplessly looked on as the gelding fought to free himself. In the background, I remember hearing a voice yelling at me to do something, although to this day I don't know if it was the horse's owner yelling or if it was my own mind telling me I had caused this mess, now it was up to me to fix it.

The problem with wrecks of this nature is they happen so quickly that you aren't allowed much time to think. In this case, I wanted desperately to rush over and try to free the leg. The thing was, I was certain if I did, the horse would panic even more and perhaps get himself into an even bigger storm.

The one thing I knew for sure was that in his eyes, this horse was in a life-and-death situation. Not only was his leg caught, but he had a predator, me, standing less than fifteen feet away. Almost out of instinct, I began to back away from him, hoping, I guess, that without the threat of my presence he might settle down enough to be able to concentrate solely on freeing the leg.

I'm not sure if that was what made the difference or if it was purely coincidence, but no sooner had I backed some distance away than he suddenly pulled the leg free. He fell over backwards, landing first on his butt, then rolling over on his right side. Almost immediately he was back on his feet and running for all he was worth with me standing in the middle of the pen like somebody who had been caught in the crosswalk of a busy intersection when the light changed.

Standing there watching that horse frantically stampede around the corral suddenly made me feel very foolish. I had gotten both me and the horse into a mess I wasn't sure I'd be able to get us out of, all because I thought I knew more than I did. I assumed that the catching technique that I used on the previous six horses would automatically work on this one. I was wrong, and now the horse was paying for my mistake.

As I stood there feeling sorry for myself and trying to get my thoughts in some kind of order, something strange happened. To be honest, I would never ask anybody to believe this, because frankly I'm not sure I believe it myself. But, I swear that just for a split second, through the dust and haze of the early evening, I saw the old man standing at the corral fence. He had a reassuring look on his face that told me this thing was going to be okay if I just settled down and tried to work from the horse's point of view. I needed to stop thinking about myself and start thinking about this horse.

A picture of what I needed to do began to form in my mind. For whatever reason, this horse was thinking that I was there to kill him, so he was literally running for his life. I needed to do something that, in his eyes, would show him that I wasn't there to harm him.

I very slowly began to cross my hands in front of me and at the same time lower my head and crouch my shoulders in an attempt to try to look as submissive as possible. I stood motionless and looking at the ground in this manner for about ten minutes before finally hearing a change in the horse's gait. He had gone from an out-of-control run to a slower lope, which he kept up for three full laps before dropping into a trot. He made only half a lap in the trot before slowing to a walk and then stopping.

Because my head was to my chest, I couldn't see where he was but from the sound his feet made when he stopped and his heavy breathing from the stress of the run, I knew he was behind me, about ten feet away, and just off my left shoulder.

I continued to stand motionless for at least five more minutes before hearing what sounded like the horse taking a step. He would take three more steps before I felt confident that he was in fact moving and moving in my direction. Apparently his fear had turned into curiosity about me, and it was now getting the better of him.

By this time the sun had gone completely down, and the horse's owner had turned on a single floodlight in one end of the corral. It threw barely enough light to cast a shadow, but at least it was better than working in the dark.

The horse continued his slow and obviously labored advance towards me. It was so slow, in fact, that it was another fifteen minutes before I knew for sure that he was within about four feet of my back. By then, I'd been standing completely motionless for over thirty minutes, and coupled with the cool air of the early evening, this had begun to cause my joints and neck to ache.

I stopped my advance and helplessly looked on.

I needed desperately to move but was afraid that if I did, I might send the horse stampeding off again, something that I didn't want to do. I decided to suck up the pain and remain motionless for a little while longer to see what might transpire.

The decision paid off. Less than five minutes later, the horse was standing quietly by my side, head low, eyes half closed, and contentedly licking his lips. It was, I thought, finally time to move. I drew a deep breath and slowly began to raise my head. Out of the corner of my eye I could see the horse's head raising too. With my head again in an upright position, I stood motionless for a few more minutes before slowly moving my left hand to my side. The horse lazily turned his head to see but otherwise seemed oblivious to the movement.

I stopped my hand briefly at my side then slowly began to raise it in the horse's direction. Watching the horse's reaction out of the corner of my eye, I stopped my hand's advance as soon as he began to show the slightest bit of concern. I then slowly moved my hand back to my side and started over.

It took nearly ten minutes before I was finally able to touch him on his neck. And even then, that was all it was—a touch. I decided at that point that that was enough for one day.

I began to move directly away from him by very slowly sidestepping to my right. After I was about five feet away, I slowly turned my back to him and nonchalantly walked away. Incredibly enough, the horse turned and followed. He stayed with me until I climbed through the rail fence, at which time he simply turned and walked back to the center of the pen and stood.

By working with him in the exact same way over the next four days, he began to show tremendous improvement. By the fifth day, I could enter the pen, and he was so comfortable with me that he would approach almost immediately. On the eighth day, he met me at the gate. I entered the pen and for the first time slipped the halter over his nose, buckled it in place, and led him around. I also brought his owner in and worked with the two of them, getting them used to each other and working on catching and leading.

I had gotten there late in the afternoon that day, and by the time we finished, it was already getting dark. The woman stayed at the pen to feed, and I decided to head for home. I got as far as the shadow of the house and couldn't help but turn around and look back at the woman and her horse. She was leaning on the corral fence, and he was contentedly munching away at his supper in the shallow beam of the flood light.

A sudden cool breeze came up which made me shiver, and for a brief second, I could have sworn I heard the old man say, "It wasn't as tough as you thought, was it?" It felt so real that I found myself looking around for him in the darkness, only to come to my senses seconds later knowing full well that he'd been dead for years.

Looking back, I think that if there is any one horse that comes to mind with any frequency, it's that one. I suppose the reason is that he was able to prove to me, beyond a shadow of a doubt, that each horse is, in fact, an individual. Just because a certain training technique works on one doesn't necessarily mean it will work on all of them. He is also the one that taught me to look for the little signals of communication that horses send, such as a flick of the tail, a certain look in the eye, and even the shifting of weight.

Over the years, I have come to understand that the little signals we often miss tell the most about the horse. Catching one of those signals has many times meant the difference between a horse that stays with me during training and one that stampedes off into the next county, like this one tried to do. Catching these signals is also a very accurate way to tell what a horse's disposition is before you even get in a pen with him. Had I taken the time to look at what that horse had been trying to tell me when I first entered his pen, chances are we could have avoided the traumatic episode that followed.

I guess it's safe to say that since my early days of what I can only call hit-and-miss training, my feel, timing, and understanding have greatly improved. This has made similar situations not only less traumatic for both the horse and myself, but a little less time consuming as well.

I have found that the key to being able to catch horses that don't want to be caught is, first, knowing why they don't want to be caught and, second, being able to change their minds. I have also found that most hard-to-catch horses fall into two major categories—spoiled or scared. Of the two, I would say that it's easier to change the mind of a spoiled horse than a scared one. The reason being is that for the most part, spoiled horses are looking for a way to avoid work. If they can't be caught, they can't be worked. As a rule, if you can make it more work for the spoiled horse not to be caught than it is to be caught, he will change his mind quickly, and thus become easy or at least easier to catch.

With a scared horse, you're dealing with a whole different set of problems. Ninety percent of these horses are afraid to be caught because of what happens to them afterward. These are usually horses that, in their minds, are physically or mentally abused while being ridden. In other words, they're handled with heavy hands, jerked around, consistently forced to do things that they aren't comfortable doing, or even forced to wear tack that doesn't fit right, causing soreness. If you tried to use the same technique catching a horse like this as you use on a spoiled horse, you'd probably end up compounding the problem and, in turn, making him even harder to catch.

Spoiled horses, as I said, are usually a little more cut-and-dried. The easiest one I ever got to work with was a twenty-two-year-old Arab mare that had been brought to one of my training clinics. The mare's owner said that she was completely impossible to catch, and in fact, it had taken nearly two hours to catch her that morning.

We went ahead and put the mare in the round pen that was set up in the middle of the rodeo arena where the clinic was being held. We left her there for about thirty minutes while the other participants registered and checked in. Following check-in, I gathered all of the participants and spectators near the round pen and explained the horse's problem. I then entered the round pen holding the horse's halter and lead rope.

As expected, the mare turned her butt towards me and slowly walked away. As I began to follow, she broke into a slow jog with her head turned out away from me, as if to say, I'm ignoring you.

I took the end of the lead rope and slapped it three times on the ground. The mare immediately broke into a fast lope. I continued to swing the rope over my head, forcing her to keep up the torrid pace as I made my way to the pen's middle.

She had made about a half dozen revolutions to the right when I cut her off and forced her back around to the left. As I made my way back to the center of the pen, I noticed out of the corner of my eye that she threw a glance in my direction. That warranted a stop on my part to reward her for a proper response, even if it was just a glance. She made about another revolution and a half before turning her whole head in my direction. I immediately began to step backwards, again rewarding her for a proper response. She took another ten steps, slowed to a stop, and turned and faced me. I backed a few more steps, stopped, and stood.

I explained to the crowd that what I was doing was trying to talk to the horse in a way that she could understand. I was trying to let her know that as long as she stood still and faced me we could both stand quietly. But if she didn't, she'd have to work and work at the pace that I dictated.

I stood for a short time, then picked a point about ten feet straight out from her hip and slowly headed for it. By the time I reached that point I was standing somewhat behind her. This is usually enough to send most spoiled horses moving away again. Much to my surprise the little horse not only didn't run, she turned and faced me, something that in similar situations usually takes fifteen to twenty minutes to accomplish. I made my way back around to her other side, and once again she faced me. Frankly, I was amazed.

"It usually doesn't go this quick," I told the crowd of astonished onlookers. I made my way to the center of the pen with the horse following quietly at my elbow. Catching this horse that had taken its owner two hours to catch earlier had taken me less than four minutes. This was, by far, the fastest it had ever gone for any horse I'd ever worked with.

Of course, in order for what we'd just done to actually mean something to the horse, we repeated the whole process several more times throughout the day. The next morning we turned the horse loose in the rodeo arena and left her there for about twenty minutes. The owner then went in to catch her. As soon as she entered the arena, the horse not only turned to face her but walked right up and allowed herself to be caught and haltered.

Apparently all this horse needed was a little direction. In her mind, the proper way to be caught was to run around for an hour or so, because that's what her owner had taught her. Once she was shown how to stand still when somebody approached, she decided that was a much easier way to go.

In complete contrast, I remember a big quarter horse mare named Cookie that was also a spoiled, hard-to-catch horse. She was, I would say, a little less willing to cooperate.

Cookie was a sixteen-year-old trail horse that had spent most of her life with a person who let her get away with anything and everything. Unfortunately, her behavior had gotten so bad that she had even gotten the better of that person's good nature, which resulted in her being sold. I was called in by her new owner, a young lady named Erin, to see if we could get her back on the right track. When I arrived at the stable where Cookie was being boarded, Erin had already put her in the round pen and was waiting for me to get there.

"She's pretty nasty," she told me, as we both stood looking at the horse from outside the pen. "I hope you can help her."

"I hope so, too," I replied, entering the round pen with halter and lead rope at the ready.

The horse responded to my presence by slowly turning her butt towards me and looking back with an expression that said, "You'll leave me alone if you know what's good for you." Then, as if to make sure I got her point, she let out a loud and heartfelt snort, followed by a flick of her tail and a stomp of her left hind foot.

I wanted to let her know that I wasn't intimidated, so I began advancing directly at her butt while at the same time slowly swinging the lead rope. She began walking away with her head cocked in my direction. Wanting to show her that I wanted her to face me, I stopped, hoping that would halt her retreat. It did, but not in a way that I'd hoped for.

She stopped, turned in my direction, pinned her ears back, and charged.

Now, of all the abilities that I've had to acquire over my years as a horse trainer, the one thing I've become really good at is twirling a lead rope. It's something that I do all the time. I twirl it when I'm standing still. I do it when I'm walking from place to place. I do it when

She stopped, turned in my direction, pinned her ears back, and charged.

I'm bored. I even do it when I don't know I'm doing it. As a result of all of this mindless lead rope twirling, I have accidentally become deadly accurate with the end of it.

Lucky for me, because as the mare charged, it was the only deterrent I had at my disposal. As her charge got closer, I aimed and consequently hit her soundly just above the left nostril with the braided end of the cotton rope. This turned her head just enough so that in the next revolution of the rope I was able to strike her on the cheek just below the ear. With the third revolution, I hit her high on the neck just behind the same ear.

The three pops with the rope were enough to stop her dead in her tracks momentarily with her head turned away from me and her body off balance. I tapped her four times on the shoulder with the spinning rope, then once on the butt as she retreated, to extinguish any thoughts she might have had about kicking at me as she left. There, I had set the ground rules. You don't attack me, and I won't defend myself, simple as that.

She headed for the rail and began running circles around me as I lightly twirled the lead rope over my head. After she made about a half dozen very fast laps, I quit twirling the rope, giving her the opportunity to stop or at least slow down if she wished. She went another three laps, slammed on the brakes, reversed direction, and took off at the same speed. I simply stood quietly in the middle and let her make up her mind as to what she wanted to do.

She made about four very fast laps before dropping into a trot for a lap or two, then a walk. Finally she stopped. She stood with her left side towards me and her head away from me, over the fence. I guess she figured that if she couldn't scare me, the least she could do was ignore me. I scuffed my foot on the ground a couple of times hoping to draw her attention my way so I could, in turn, reward her. It didn't work. I then jingled some change in my pocket. No good.

I sidestepped to my left to make it easier for her to see me. She simply turned her head farther to the right. Once again, I began to make my way towards her rear, taking up a position about six feet straight out from her hip. I scuffed my foot on the ground to see if perhaps now I might be able to get her attention. She simply began to walk away. So I, in turn, went back to swinging the rope, which consequently sent her back into a fast run.

I went back to the middle of the pen and let her go to work. Over the next thirty minutes, she stopped several times, but not once did she offer to look in my direction. I could tell that she was becoming exhausted so I began to make an effort to let her know that she had worked hard enough. I completely quit twirling the rope, and each time she stopped I would let her stand for several minutes before I did anything. Still, she refused to look at me and chose running off instead of standing still.

Finally, after forty-five minutes of running at full speed, she stopped and threw an ever-so-slight glance in my direction. I immediately rewarded her by stepping backwards about five feet. For the first time that day, instead of putting her head over the rail, the mare was holding it straight. She still wasn't looking directly at me, but at least she wasn't trying to completely ignore me either.

At this point, I was standing about twenty feet away from her, straight out from her right shoulder. After letting her stand for about three minutes, I slowly began to sidestep to my left, towards her rear. As I did, she finally gave me the response I'd been looking for. Her head began to turn in my direction, and I began stepping backwards. As I did, her head came completely around until she was looking directly at me.

A look of resignation came over her as her head lowered and she sleepily licked her lips. I'd seen this look thousands of times on other hard-to-catch horses. She was, in a sense, telling me that she now was ready to listen to what I had to say. In any other case, this is where I would finally begin to work with the horse, teaching it how to face me when I approached and consequently being able to have it follow me. But I felt it was clear that she'd had enough for one day.

Wanting to end on a positive note, I slowly approached her, stopping and standing periodically, hopefully to reinforce the fact that I didn't want her to run away. After a short time, I was standing about two feet from her shoulder. I stood quietly for a few seconds then slowly reached up and stroked her on her neck. She relaxed even more by cocking her left hind foot on the ground.

I then left the pen to let her rest and cool off for about thirty minutes. When I finally came back to get her, she very quietly turned and approached me, meeting me in the center of the pen. I slipped her halter on, lavishly petted her neck and shoulders, and gave the lead rope to Erin, who returned her to her pen.

The problem with Cookie, and other horses that are that bad off, is that even after a day as exhausting as the one she had just had, she will probably be just as bad the next day. In fact, it's not uncommon for a terribly spoiled horse to take a week or more finally to decide for itself that it's easier to stand and be caught than it is to run away. Even then, I have seen horses, two or three months down the road, suddenly revert back to not wanting to be caught. The good part is that if they do, usually all it takes to bring them back around is a simple flick of the lead rope. They then run off a few feet, stop and face you with a look that says, "What was I thinking?"

Now the thing about most spoiled horses is that when they move away from you, they're doing it purely as an evasive action to avoid work. Whereas, in the case of a frightened horse, moving away is usually a reaction to their flight instinct telling them that you are there to harm them. Naturally, they want to get as far away from you as they can to avoid what they perceive as a threat.

By using the exact same technique on a frightened horse as you would on a spoiled one, chances are you would just reinforce his fears and, in turn, make him even harder to catch. On the other hand, if you can gain the horse's trust while using his flight instinct to your advantage, you will find you'll be much further ahead. At least that's what I have found.

The one horse that comes to mind is a little gelding named Mac. Mac was an unbroke four-year-old that had been abused by his owner's husband for about a year. His owner, who had since divorced the guy and moved to Colorado from Texas, called me to see if I'd be interested in training him.

When I first saw the little horse, there were two things about him that impressed me right away. The first was his coloring. He was a liver chestnut with a flaxen mane and tail, three white stockings, and a blaze on his face. The other was that he was absolutely terrified, especially of men.

He was standing in a 12-by-24-foot run at a boarding stable when I came to see him. His owner had been unable to catch him since she put him in the pen three weeks earlier. If I was going to work with him, I was first going to have to catch him.

As I entered the gate into his pen, the horse panicked and began to run, looking for a way out. I stood quietly by the gate as the horse frantically paced back and forth at the other end of the rectangular pen. I stood by the gate for nearly fifteen minutes before the horse finally stopped, head over the fence, butt towards me, and shaking with fear like he was freezing to death.

I remained by the gate for another five minutes before he finally began showing slight signs of settling down. It was obvious, though, that he had absolutely no intention of getting anywhere near me. So, in an effort to get some movement from him, I began to slowly move towards him, walking close to the left side of the pen and leaving him the entire right side of the pen as an escape route, which he quickly chose to use.

Soon, I was standing quietly in the middle of the pen with one hand in my pocket, the other holding the halter and lead rope, as he ran circles around me. The little horse ran nonstop for the next twenty minutes, first one direction, then the other, with his head over the top rail of the corral fence the entire time. Soon after that, however, I think he started to realize that even though my simply being in the pen with him was frightening, I hadn't made any aggressive moves or actions towards him. This allowed his flight instinct to begin to diminish, and in its place, curiosity began to grow.

Finally he stopped and, with his head still over the fence, began to throw quick and cautious glances in my direction. I, in turn, began to take steps backwards to relieve some of the pressure he was feeling. After about five minutes of intermittent glances, he finally turned and looked directly at me. I backed up even farther, which caused him actually to shift his weight in my direction. I backed up far enough to where I was right up against the opposite side of the corral. With him still looking in my direction, I simply climbed out of the corral and left him there to ponder what had just happened.

I returned about an hour later and began the whole process over. This time, within about ten minutes, he was not only looking at me, but facing me as well. On that note, I left the corral again. About a half hour later, I entered the corral and stood quietly by the gate. This time he didn't even offer to move, but rather turned to face me. At that point, I figured that was enough for one day.

The next day when I entered his pen, he took off running just as he had the day before, only this time he made only three revolutions around the pen before coming to a stop less than six feet away from me. I immediately began to back away, and he quietly began to follow. After a few paces, I stopped to see if perhaps he would continue towards me, but when I stopped, so did he. Nevertheless, I remained standing where I was and after only a few short minutes, he slowly began to inch his way towards me. Within five minutes, I turned to walk away, and he followed.

By later that afternoon, I was not only able to approach him, but I could also slip a halter on and off his nose, buckle it in place, and lead him around the corral. Now I suppose, if I wanted to, I could have passed off what we had just accomplished as my having some fantastic insight into the horse's mind, an insight that is so complicated most people couldn't even begin to understand it. The truth of the matter is, if I can do it, anybody can do it.

There is nothing magical about catching a horse that doesn't want to be caught. It's just a matter of understanding why he doesn't want to, and then knowing what it takes to change his mind. Put simply, it's making the horse comfortable enough with you that being caught is no big deal. Of course, that may also involve altering the way he's handled once he's caught. But, what the heck. If you've taken the time to teach the horse how to be caught, showing him that life isn't as tough as he thought afterwards isn't much more work.

In fact, it could be as simple as catching the horse and then tying him in a shady place instead of riding him or catching him, grooming him, and turning him loose. Let him know that just because he's being caught, it doesn't necessarily mean he's going to have to work. That way, when the time does come to work, he'll probably be happier to perform for you.

These were my thoughts as I made my way to my truck following the well-known trainer's demonstrations on catching hard-to-catch horses. As I climbed into the cab, I turned and looked back at my fellow spectators. As far as I could tell, about twelve of them were now proud new owners of the trainer's specially designed lead rope.

Several of them were standing in the parking lot trying the ropes out. Ropes were being twirled everywhere. One fellow knocked his own hat off with his. A lady, trying to get the feel of hers, accidentally whacked her husband in the crotch.

I couldn't help but shake my head as I drove away thinking about all of the horses standing in their paddocks at home totally unsuspecting of the wrath that was about to descend upon them. I also couldn't help but wonder how long it was going to take for the magic to wear off those ropes, and how many horses, if any, were actually going to be helped. Moreover, I wondered how many wouldn't be.

NOTES FOR CATCHING THE UNCATCHABLE HORSE

There are several things concerning this chapter I'd like to comment on, and I guess it might be best to just start at the beginning. I began and ended this chapter by talking about a trainer I had seen who was selling lead ropes as part of a demonstration he was doing, and I guess I wasn't too subtle about trying to hide the way I felt about it.

While part of my motivation was to warn people about the difference between substance and flash, I realize now it could have been done in a much more productive manner. Unfortunately, at the time I was still a few years away from being able to see that the more time a person spends criticizing others, the less time he has to work on improving his own craft.

Another thing I was interested in seeing were the words I used to describe certain behavior in horses. In particular the use of the word "spoiled." I also pointed out during the chapter that at the time, I believed a spoiled horse to be "one that tries to get out of work."

This is a subject where my thoughts have changed dramatically over the years. I have come to believe that pretty much any behavior horses exhibit around humans was in one way or another installed by a human . . . including being hard to catch. The horse is simply repeating behavior it was taught. In other words, in the horse's mind, the behavior itself has no value. It does, however, have value to us due to the fact that we attach words like "bad" or "good" or "spoiled" to it. Those words have emotion attached to them so when using them we are already emotional in some way about the behavior. It is then much easier to place fault or blame to the behavior, which often puts us in a "me against the horse" frame of mind, which in turn can negatively affect the training we offer the horse.

Which brings me to the next point. One of the things I also talk about in this chapter is how I used to make it more work for a horse that didn't want to be caught than it would be for him to stand still. I suppose one could say it was very similar to the popular horse training idea of making the wrong thing difficult and the right thing easy. This is also one of those things that, over the years, I have had the opportunity to rethink.

Somewhere along the line I have come to the understanding that not only is the wrong thing apparently already difficult for most troubled horses (otherwise they probably wouldn't be troubled to begin with), but so is the right thing. So rather than making the wrong thing even harder for them, I decided to try and find ways to bring the overall anxiety level down so I can then guide and/or direct the horse to the desired response.

Now when I work with a hard-to-catch horse I'm more apt to do less chasing (or as I put it in the chapter, dictating the horse's speed) and more teaching. This is usually done in the form of showing the horse how to turn and look at someone who is approaching rather than the horse turning their hindquarters toward them and running off. Overall, I've found this to be a much less adversarial way of working with the horse, less stressful for everybody involved, and less time-consuming overall.

Ground manners

We had just finished driving through some of the prettiest country in Colorado. Unfortunately, we were on one of the worst roads in Colorado, too. The fact that we were right in the middle of a late spring thaw made the road even more treacherous, with large, water-filled potholes, long patches of thick, slippery ice, and miles and miles of greasy mud.

We crossed the last of four cattle guards and came to a stop in the 425-acre pasture with about sixty head of horses on it. As I scanned the one-lane dirt road that stretched out in front of us for a spot large enough to get the truck and trailer turned around, Susie Heide, my help that day, searched the herd for the horse we had come to pick up, a sorrel mare named Sugar.

I had recently bought the horse from a lady who could no longer afford to keep her. We had traveled the eleven miles on this deserted back road to the secluded high mountain pasture where Sugar was being kept so that we could move her to better pasture. The winter had been unforgiving in the high country that year, and although the pasture that the horses were on was indeed large, it simply couldn't sustain them adequately. Because the road was often snowed in, no one had been able to get back there to feed them. As a result, all sixty head, including Sugar, were quite thin.

Having seen Sugar's condition a couple of weeks earlier when I purchased her, I decided to take her off this pasture as soon as I could get a trailer in. We were going to move her to a pasture on the plains where winter had long since disappeared and the grass was already ankle deep and summer green.

"There she is," Susie said, looking across the pasture at the herd. "Next to that paint."

"I see her," I replied. "If you want to go get her caught up, I'll see if I can get the truck turned around."

"Okay," she said, grabbing the halter off the seat and sliding out the door.

I'd known Susie for about three years at that time and had found her to be an excellent horse person—very quiet, patient, and knowledgeable. So, as I began to slip and slide my truck down the road, I didn't even give a second thought to the fact that she might have trouble catching the little mare. I traveled about two miles farther down the road before finding a place large enough and dry enough to get my four-wheel-drive, extended cab GMC, with trailer attached, turned around. By the time I returned to where the herd was, I could see Susie clear across the pasture, about a quarter mile away, waving her arms at me. Above her in the trees, I could see the mare trotting up the side of the mountain.

I hope this isn't going to take too long, I remember thinking to myself as I grabbed my lariat off the back seat and headed out across the pasture. There were only about three hours of daylight left.

Over the past three years, Susie and I had worked together on almost a daily basis. We had been involved in so many problem-horse situations that nothing was really out of the ordinary for us anymore. It had gotten to the point that when situations like this came up, we simply shrugged our shoulders and went out and got the job done, often without even having to communicate verbally.

From my vantage point in the pasture, I could see that Sugar had run into the pasture's south fence line, which was only about one hundred yards up the hill from where Susie was standing. She was now following the fence line west, away from Susie.

The good news was that about three hundred yards away was the pasture's west fence line. If Sugar continued in the direction she was traveling, she would soon be in the corner where the two lines met. If we took our time and were patient about how we did this, catching her could be pretty easy.

I began to take an angle towards the corner. Susie began to head up the hill, following Sugar's trail. We both came out of the trees at the same time and entered a small clearing. There in front of us was Sugar, quietly standing in the southwest corner of the pasture.

Instinctively we both stopped so as to limit the amount of pressure our presence would cause the horse. She looked at both of us but for the most part appeared to be resigned to the fact that she was now caught. She wasn't a hard-to-catch horse in the true sense, but as we were about to learn, she did lack some in other areas.

Because of where we were when we came into the little clearing, by luck I happened to be about twenty feet closer to the mare than Susie was. As a result, I was the first to approach her. She stood quietly and allowed me to walk up without incident. As I slowly slipped the loop of the lariat over her head, Susie began to approach with the halter.

With Susie still more than fifty feet away, the horse just matter-of-factly began to walk down the hill as if I wasn't even there. I put a little tension on the rope around her neck to remind her that she was caught. She completely ignored the pressure and continued walking. In order to try to stop her forward movement, I grabbed ahold of the rope with both hands and planted my feet. Instead of stopping, however, she broke into a trot, pulling me down the hill as she went.

The rope had by now slipped all the way through my hands so that I was holding on precariously to its knotted end, but I was still managing a pretty good imitation of an anchor. That is, until I hit a large patch of snow, which caused me to lose my footing. It was about that same time that Sugar decided to break into a lope, making me look like something fresh out of a Three Stooges movie. Still holding on with all my might, I was now running faster than any person has the right to. She was pulling me in such a way that my stride was about thirty feet long, and any wrong move on my part would cause me to have a spectacular wreck.

As I rocketed down the hill, my only thought was to try somehow to get my end of the rope dallied around a tree, which would definitely stop the mare and hopefully not cause her or me any injury. Now, I'm sure we passed a bunch of trees on the way down, but to tell the truth, we were simply moving too fast for me to do anything other than keep my balance.

We were nearing the bottom of the hill when I looked up and saw a rock the size of a '39 Hudson just off to the right. At the speed and trajectory that I was traveling, if I didn't let go, the whole thing would end in disaster, especially for Susie who would have had to scrape me off the rock. With discretion being the better part of valor and not wanting to be the next passenger for Flight-For-Life, I let go of the rope.

The entire incident from start to finish had taken less than twenty seconds. As my momentum carried me head over heels down the remainder of the hill and deposited me in the open meadow of the pasture, I could have sworn it took longer. Susie came running down the hill, sliding to a stop only a few feet away, laughing so hard I thought she would wet herself.

"You okay?" she asked, trying to catch her breath.

"Yeah," I replied, squinting through the one eye that didn't have dirt in it.

"Sorry to laugh," she chuckled, "but that looked really funny."

"I bet it did," I said, crawling over to my hat, which lay dented and bent a short distance away. I stood up, slapping the dirt and snow off my jeans with the hat, then trying to straighten the kinks out of it while Susie, still laughing, brushed the snow from my back.

"She sure isn't much on manners, is she?" Susie asked, as we watched the mare run hell bent for election towards the rest of the herd.

"No, she sure isn't," I replied.

The "manners" that Susie mentioned is a term we sometimes use, referring to a horse's respect, or lack thereof, for people in the animal's general vicinity. This horse had been pretty blatant about her lack of respect as she walked away from me with my rope around her neck.

Admittedly, I'm sure that my awkward and out-of-control presence behind her added to her not wanting to stop once she took off running. But that doesn't excuse the fact that she took it upon herself to leave in the first place and then didn't respond to my initial request to stop.

Now the thing is, the horse can't be blamed for this lack of respect or ground manners. As a rule, horses are born with an almost complete lack of these manners, not just towards people but towards just about everything around them. If you ever take the time to watch the way baby horses act, you will see that they do an awful lot of running into one another. They also think nothing of running into, over, or under their mothers at any given time.

As babies, this behavior is almost completely accepted by the herd. It may even be a year or two down the road before other horses begin to reprimand them for doing it. However, the fact remains that, sooner or later, the herd will teach the babies some manners.

Babies act the same with people. If we don't take the time to teach them how to act when we're near, they end up grown horses that drag us down hills, walk all over us, or refuse to lead when asked. It's up to us to explain to them what we expect when we're near. If we don't, they'll simply never know.

The question is, how do we teach the horse ground manners? Well, most of the time it's simply a matter of teaching the horse how to give to pressure. Let's take Sugar, for instance. We found that her biggest problem was that she had no real understanding of what to do when somebody applied pressure to her, whether it was asking her to stop, back up, or even step over. With her, we had to start from scratch.

We began by teaching her how to stop while being led. For most horses this comes as second nature. In fact, they often are taught how to stop before they learn how to lead. But for Sugar, it apparently had been part of her training that had been completely overlooked. Aside from our little excursion down the mountainside, this problem also became very clear a couple of months later when I was taking her from the corral into the barn.

As I was leading her the short distance, I stopped to pick up a piece of baling twine that I noticed on the ground. Sugar simply ignored the fact that I was no longer moving and kept right on walking, actually dragging me about three feet before stopping.

This was as good a time as any to start fixing this little problem, I thought. I took hold of the lead rope and applied light, constant pressure downwards and slightly back, without pulling on her. She responded by leaning into the pressure. Obviously this is not what I was looking for, so I met her resistance with some resistance of my own. Again, I was not pulling on her but rather putting the same amount of pressure on her that she was putting on me. This went on for a very short time before she started tossing her head in search of a way to get rid of the pressure. When that didn't work, she tried to walk through the pressure. When that didn't work, she finally flexed, giving in to the pressure.

Immediately I released my hold on the rope, giving her a very clear and noticeable reward for the proper response. I let her stand for a minute, then did the whole thing over. This time she tossed her head only a couple of times before once again flexing. Again she received an immediate reward. We repeated this until I could apply very light pressure on the lead rope and she would flex immediately. When I was confident that she completely understood what I was asking, we went a step further.

I applied light pressure on the rope, causing her to flex nicely, only this time I didn't release the pressure. I could feel her sticking her nose out ever so slightly and leaning on me as if to say, "Hey, where's my reward?" As she began flexing, the additional pressure also caused her to lean ever so slightly backwards. This is what I was looking for, so once again I released the pressure.

I let her stand for a short time, then applied the pressure again. This time, as if some big light went on in her head, she not only flexed, but actually took two steps backwards. In less than ten minutes from when we started, Sugar had learned how to back, responding to only light pressure on the lead rope. Only when I was sure she completely understood what I wanted did I lead her forward again.

When we finally did go forward, it was only a couple of steps before I applied the pressure to ask her to stop. Apparently unsure of herself, she began leaning on me. After only a couple of steps, however, the light went on, and she flexed, stopped, and backed.

We continued to work on this for the next thirty minutes, moving forward a little farther each time before stopping and backing. By the end of that time, I didn't even have to put pressure on the lead rope to stop her. She had become so conditioned to stopping when I stopped that she just did whenever I did. By the end of that day, she had become so well mannered that I couldn't believe she was the same horse that had dragged me down the hillside only two months earlier.

Sugar is a pretty common example of a horse with poor ground manners. Often all it takes to fix the problem is teaching the horse to give to pressure. I have also seen horses that knew perfectly well how to give to pressure, but for whatever reason simply didn't want to. In those cases, the horse has less of a training problem and more of an attitude problem. Specifically, the horse has a lack of respect for people.

Tom was one such horse. Tom was a big, bay quarter horse that I'd been asked to work with because he had simply become too hard for his owner to handle. It wasn't that he was doing anything particularly mean; it's just that he had developed a general lack of respect and would not bother to respond to cues when asked. This was not only obvious in his ground manners but while being ridden as well.

His problem was apparent to me the first time I led him out of the pasture he was being boarded in. I stopped to close the pasture gate, and he bullied his way past me, throwing his head and jerking me off balance. He then dragged me about five yards to where there was a small patch of green grass and shoved his nose down in it.

I asked him to bring his head up by applying light pressure upwards. There was no response. I then used a little more pressure. Again, no response. Finally I pulled on him with everything I had. He didn't even flinch. This horse had discovered the one thing that we hope horses never figure out. That is that they are bigger and stronger than us. He knew that he could keep his head down there as long as he wanted, because I didn't have the power it takes to get him to bring it back up. At least that's what he thought.

Horses have several areas on their bodies that are sensitive to touch, but none more so than the area around the nose and mouth. I decided to make it uncomfortable for him to have that very sensitive area of his on the ground. As he contentedly munched away on the grass, I again applied light pressure to the lead rope, asking him to raise his head.

As expected, he ignored my request. I then slid my foot over close to his bottom lip and, while still applying light pressure on the rope, tapped the lip with my toe. This was by no means a forceful kick but rather a meaningful tap, similar to that which you would use if tapping someone on the shoulder to get his attention. His head sprang up immediately, and there was an expression of complete surprise on his face.

I began to pet him on his neck to reward him for bringing his head up but even before I could get two strokes in, he was returning his head to the ground. I began to apply upward pressure, asking him not to put his head down there, but again he ignored me. That is, until his nose reached the ground and was met by the toe of my boot. Again, it sprang up instantly.

I decided to remove the temptation of the grass by leading him away from it. Even that was of no use. He simply jerked his head back down into the grass as I tried to walk away. Again, he ran into the toe of my boot. This time, however, I tapped him a little more soundly in an effort to let him know that now I meant business.

His head popped up like I'd hit him with a hot shot. I began to pet him to let him know that as long as his head was up, he'd get a reward. As I was petting him, he halfheartedly thought about returning his head to the grass. I asked him not to by applying light pressure to the lead rope. This time his head came back up.

As I began to lead him from the pasture to the barn, another little problem arose. He wanted to go to the barn a little faster than I did. Well, actually, a lot faster than I did. As we walked, nearly his entire body was in front of me so that, in a sense, he was leading me. Obviously this is unacceptable. Unfortunately, he ignored my requests to slow down. In an effort to get him to slow to the speed I was walking, I decided that first I needed to get him to stop so we could start out at the same speed. The problem was that he was ignoring my requests to stop as well.

Finally, I simply stopped in my tracks, brought his head around, and allowed him to walk in circles around me until he decided to stop on his own. He circled about seven times before finally stopping. I allowed him to stand quietly for a few seconds before starting out again.

When we did, he immediately picked up his blistering pace. Again, I stopped and allowed him to circle. We repeated this countless times, and still he made no effort to slow down or stop when I asked. I found this unusual because in every other case that I'd had like this, the horse usually got the message within a very short time. But this horse simply had other ideas. As I saw it, I needed to make a point and that point was that I wanted him to behave himself and stop dragging me around. The question was, how would I make that point?

His head popped up like I'd hit him with a hot shot.

I knew that I needed to make this horse uncomfortable enough when he moved in front of me that he simply wouldn't want to do it anymore. That was the catch. How would I do that with the limited resources I had at my immediate disposal?

Finally it came to me. In the horse's eyes, there had never been any negative consequence to his headstrong actions, except perhaps his having to drag somebody around from place to place. That took a little more of his energy, but for a big horse like him, it was really no big deal. What I decided to do was correct him in a manner similar to the one I used to get his head off the ground, making it so miserable for him to do it that it simply wasn't an option anymore.

As we started out this time, he began right away to pick up his quickened pace. I asked him to slow down with pressure on the lead rope. As expected, he ignored the pressure and began to walk past me. This time, I quickly brought his head around and began to poke him in the ribs with the tips of my fingers. He didn't like that at all and ran a couple of quick circles around me with me poking him as he went.

He had a completely different look on his face when he came to a stop that time. It was evident that I'd gotten his attention. We had to repeat this about four times before he finally began to respond to my requests to slow down when I applied pressure with the lead rope. By the time we reached the barn, he had finally decided to lead like a gentleman. While I'd begun to make an impression on him that day, it took another two days of the same type of handling before he was consistently being a good boy.

Now I feel that I should point out here that when I was poking him in the ribs, I was doing so as an irritant rather than a punishment. I also tried to be as consistent as I possibly could when I did it. What I mean by that is that I tried to catch him at the very same time each time he began to pass me. I also tried to use the same amount of force each time, which wasn't much, and I tried to stop as soon as he showed me that he'd had enough.

By being consistent, the horse soon learned that once he passed a certain point, life became pretty uncomfortable. If he never reached that point, life stayed pretty good. He had simply made up his mind that he didn't want to be miserable.

Since being forced to use that technique on old Tom, I have not only used it on horses with similar leading problems, but also on horses that seem to have no respect for people's immediate space. These are the horses that continuously walk all over you when they're being led, are all the time bumping into you as if they don't see you, or are constantly leaning on you.

Of course, just as in Tom's case, I don't automatically start out using that technique. On the contrary, I usually use it only as a last resort. For instance, most horses that are "leaners" respond rather quickly to you simply sticking an elbow out. Anytime they get too

The horse took off across the pen, squealing, bucking, and jumping.

close they run into a bony elbow. This in itself is usually enough to stop them from wanting to get too near you.

Now, while I'm on the subject of ill-mannered horses, there is another situation that comes to mind. I'd been called to a very high-class boarding stable to see a horse that had all of the symptoms of having poor ground manners. The horse was a fifteen-year-old registered paint that was being kept in a box stall inside the barn.

I stood in the aisle and watched as his owner went in the stall, caught him, and began leading him outside to a large turnout area. The horse's manners definitely left something to be desired. He was so bad, in fact, that he was borderline uncontrollable, and his owner, a fellow about 5 feet 8 inches and 150 pounds, had everything he could do just to get him out there.

The man put the horse in the turnout area and had no sooner unclipped the lead rope from the halter than the horse took off across the pen, squealing, bucking, and jumping.

"See what I mean?" the man asked, brushing off the sand that the horse had just kicked up on his shirt. "I can't hardly handle him anymore."

"How long has he been like this?" I asked.

"A couple of months," he replied.

"What's he being fed?"

"Fed?" the man questioned. "What's that got to do with anything?"

"It could have everything to do with it," I told him.

"I don't know," he shrugged. "The same thing the rest of the horses are getting, I guess."

"Let's find out."

We went into the barn and spoke with the owner of the facility. She told us that the horse was getting three pounds of fourteen percent-protein grain in the morning with two flakes of alfalfa hay, and the same thing at night. In other words, six pounds of high-energy grain per day, plus more energy-filled hay. He was also being handled and turned out only three or four times a week for an hour or less each time.

"You don't need me," I told the man. "Just get him off of that high-powered feed and get him some more exercise. In a week or so you'll have your old horse back."

I couldn't even begin to count the number of horses I've seen that were in the same boat—being fed a tremendous amount of high-powered feed, getting little or no exercise, then having owners who wonder why they're so uncontrollable and ultimately blaming the horse.

Well, the truth of the matter is, horses seldom develop problems on their own. On the contrary, most problems they develop are due to their training, or lack thereof. It's just easier to blame the horse than the trainer, especially if you're the one doing the training. A real good example is a horse that doesn't lead. These aren't the ones that push you around or walk past you as you're leading them, but rather ones that don't lead at all. The ones that don't go forward when asked.

The worst horse I ever worked with that had this problem was a gelding named Skip. He was a three-year-old whose training had been held up due to the fact that he couldn't be led out of his corral. His owner had tried everything he knew to teach the horse to lead, but to this point, nothing had worked. The only way he could lead the horse from one place to another was to pony him from another horse or have somebody behind him with a whip constantly flicking it at his heels.

When I arrived to have a look at the horse, I found him standing by himself in a large pen. He was easy to approach and halter and actually led a few feet when I asked him to. But that was about it. After leading only a short distance, he simply locked up and refused to go any farther. I moved his head quite a ways to the side to try to get some movement in his front end. This did move the front feet but nothing else. He was quite content to stand in one place and really had no ambition to go anywhere else.

For the next thirty minutes I tried everything I knew to coax the horse forward. Nothing worked. It was very clear that this horse wasn't at all frightened, but rather was completely unmotivated. In his mind, he saw absolutely no reason why he should have to follow me. Unless another horse was pulling him or someone was prodding him from behind with a whip, he was perfectly content to stand in that spot. He figured if he stood still long enough, sooner or later whoever was pulling on his head to try to move him forward would quit, and he could go back to standing in the shade.

Frankly, I was almost ready to let him do just that when suddenly an idea came to me. To this point I'd been concentrating on getting the horse to move forward. While doing this, I found that I was the one doing all the work. I'd been moving his head from side to side, pulling him in circles trying to get some movement out of him, even tapping him on the butt with the end of the lead rope. On the other hand, he wasn't working at all and, in fact, looked like he was sleeping most of the time.

It came to me that perhaps if he suddenly found that standing still when he should be leading was to become miserable, then going forward when he was asked might not seem like such a bad idea. Obviously, in order to make him miserable or get him to work, I first had to get him to move. I knew that going forward was out of the question, but I hadn't asked him to go backwards yet. That, I soon found, was the key.

I once again asked him to come forward, and once again he ignored my request. This time, however, I immediately began to shake the lead rope vigorously while walking directly at him and making a loud hissing sound through my teeth. Surprised, he quickly began to backpedal as fast as he could. We had backed about fifteen feet when I finally stopped him. It was clear that I now had his attention.

I let him stand quietly for a few seconds, then once again asked him to come forward. No response. I released the pressure and tried again. Again nothing. This time I responded by moving him backwards about twenty feet as fast as he could go. After stopping, I petted him on his neck to let him know that I wasn't doing this because I was mad, but because I needed him to do something and he wasn't trying.

As I stepped forward to ask him to lead, he halfheartedly offered some forward movement. At that, I gave him lavish praise and let him stand a little longer. When I asked him to move, he cautiously gave me two steps. Again he received a lot of praise. For the next twenty minutes, each time he even offered to come forward when asked, I praised him like he'd just won the Triple Crown. If there was no offer, he backed up and did so in a way that was completely miserable for him.

Pretty soon he was leading all over that corral. As we walked, I would let him hesitate and even stop his forward movement as long as he started walking again by the time I reached the end of the lead rope. If I hit the end of the lead rope to the point where all the slack had come out and he was now pulling on me, I would suddenly fling myself back in his direction. This would, in turn, force him backwards again. It wasn't long before he had decided that it was a lot easier to follow when asked than to stop or even offer to stop. In fact, his turnaround was so complete that the slightest pressure on the lead rope would get him moving forward.

This is not a technique that I would use on just any horse. If used on a horse that was scared to begin with, you'd probably end up losing the horse. It is also a technique that would absolutely not work on colts under the age of about two. The reason I say that is during the first two years of a horse's life, we should be making every effort to gain the animal's trust. Not that we shouldn't be doing that during the rest of his life, too, but it's particularly important during those first two formative years. How can we gain the horse's trust during that time if we're using techniques specifically designed to frighten him, even a little bit?

There are a lot of folks out there who don't feel that good ground manners are all that important. Well, I disagree. Every horse that I've ever seen that had bad manners lacked one of two things: training or respect. Because of that, the horses also had trouble trusting their handlers, which usually generated even more problems.

The old man told me years ago that if you don't have a horse's trust, you don't have anything. I have found that to be very true. I have also found that if they don't trust you on

Surprised, he quickly began to backpedal as fast as he could.

the ground, they sure won't trust you on their backs. In order to gain that trust, you've got to have a solid foundation to work from. A horse with good ground manners may not always be perfect in other respects, but at least it's a start on that foundation.

NOTES FOR GROUND MANNERS

Reading this chapter was interesting to me for a couple of reasons. First, it has been so long since I've used any of the techniques I spoke about when writing the chapter that I had actually forgotten I'd even used them! At any rate, and as with the last chapter, I am much more apt these days to try and find ways of helping a horse understand what I'm asking of it, rather than making the wrong thing "miserable," as was pointed out in the chapter.

The second thing I found interesting was the use of the words "respect" or "disrespect" throughout the chapter to describe a horse that was having trouble understanding what was expected of it.

I had only begun hearing the word respect in relation to working with horses just a few years before writing this book. It wasn't a word that resonated with me when it came to applying it to horses simply because I never believed horses were respectful or disrespectful animals to begin with. "Respect" is a human term used to describe a completely human notion of how we should treat one another.

At any rate, I recall having a discussion with my editor at the time as to whether or not we should use the term to describe certain horses' behavior or attitudes in the book. I wanted to use the words "understand" or "understanding" (such as "the horse had a lack of *understanding* of how to act around people") but my editor thought most people would resonate better with the word "respect" and changed the word throughout the book so I could see how it read (such as "the horse had a lack of respect when around people"). We discussed this on several occasions during the writing of the book, and I finally settled on the word "understanding" as the descriptive and asked my editor to leave it at that, to which he agreed.

However, it was only after the book had been released that we both realized the word "respect" had been left in, and by that time it was too late to change it. I had always meant to redo it before subsequent printings were released, but simply never got around to it.

I should also add that this is the chapter many people tell me made them laugh the hardest. For some reason, the visual of me being pulled down the hill by Sugar at the beginning of the chapter is apparently more than most folks can take. I'm really glad it has brought a smile to so many faces.

Picking up feet

Once I received an eight-year-old Morgan gelding that, the owner said, had become horrible about picking up his feet. If she tried to pick up one of his front feet, he would immediately take the foot away and backpedal as fast as he could. Anyone unfortunate enough to be holding the horse's lead rope at the time found his arms nearly ripped out of their sockets while being pulled through the dust cloud the horse made while backing.

Picking up a back foot was even more perilous. He would kick at you with such speed and agility that it was nearly impossible to get out of the way of the lightning-fast hoof. The horse's problem had become so bad that his owner could no longer find a farrier who was willing to work on him. As a result, she decided to bring him to me to see if I could work the problem out of him.

"You have my permission to do whatever it takes," she told me. "He's no good to me this way." I took that statement to mean that she expected me to get heavy-handed with him. In other words, find a way to force him into picking his feet up, whether he was comfortable doing it or not.

I tried to explain to the woman that I thought his problem was that, for whatever reason, he'd had a breakdown of trust when it came to working with his feet. Having watched his violent reaction to a farrier who had tried to work with him, it appeared that he was simply trying to defend himself, not be mean.

"Trying to bully him into picking his feet up will make matters worse," I warned. "What we need to do first is try to get his trust back, then work through the problem by making him comfortable with what we're doing."

"Whatever," she grunted, "as long as it's done within thirty days."

"It may take longer than thirty days," I told her.

"It might," she said, "but thirty days is all I'm going to stick in him. If he doesn't come around by then, he's going down the road."

I guess you can't get any plainer than that. Either this horse's problem would be gone in thirty days or the horse would be. I couldn't help thinking what a shame it would be to have to get rid of this horse simply because he had trouble picking up his feet. He was very well trained in every other way and extremely well built with almost perfect conformation. He was also quite easy to handle and even-tempered, except about his feet.

Having seen this horse's reaction to somebody trying to pick up his feet on several different occasions, I had noticed that he appeared to be trying to get away. It was when he couldn't that he became defensive and protective, using his feet to strike and kick at whomever was trying to work with him.

Knowing this, I decided to try something a little different. It was obvious that he was extremely uncomfortable with somebody handling his feet. He was so uncomfortable that his flight instinct would kick in whenever anybody tried. I wondered what would happen if I allowed him to use his flight instinct, instead of trying to hold him. In other words, I would work him without restraints in a round pen. If he decided he was under enough pressure to where he needed to run away, I would let him. Of course, I would then put additional pressure on him as he was running to make it more work for him to leave me than it was to stay.

Hopefully he would decide that, no matter how frightening it was to have someone touching his lower legs, it wasn't nearly the work running away was. This, in turn, might allow us the time we would need, first, to find the cause of his problem, and second, to work through it.

I put the horse in the round pen, removed his halter and left him alone for about fifteen minutes. I did this to allow him to become comfortable with the pen. That way, he wouldn't be gawking around when we were trying to work. I've found that it's much easier to keep a horse's attention if he's not investigating his surroundings while we're working. He will see just about everything there is to see in a round pen in about fifteen to twenty minutes and then be ready to work.

When I entered the pen, he was quietly standing in the center. I approached him without any problem whatsoever and began to pet him on his head, neck, and shoulders. I did that for about five minutes before slowly beginning to work my way down his leg. I got only a short distance below his elbow joint when I noticed he was beginning to become concerned. I then worked my way back up to his neck and shoulder, areas that were not a problem for him, before returning back to the elbow.

It took at least another four minutes to get past the elbow to where I could pet his forearm. Again he showed great concern and again I retreated back to the neck and shoulder. It took several more minutes to work past the forearm. By the time I'd gotten to his knee, however, the pressure was too much for him, and he suddenly exploded. He took off running like I was standing there with a chain saw ready to cut his leg off.

I immediately began to swing the lead rope that I'd been holding, which forced him to run even harder. He sprinted around the pen like he was in the Kentucky Derby and did so for a good five minutes. Finally I stopped swinging the rope, and he stopped running. Out of breath, he slowly turned and faced me. As I began to back up, he walked directly at me, coming to a stop near the middle of the pen. I let him rest quietly for a few seconds before starting all over from the beginning.

It took nearly forty-five minutes of working in the same manner before he would stand and allow me to run my hand the entire length of his leg. It was obvious that the incident had caused him great stress and that the only reason he was allowing me to touch the leg at all was that he was exhausted from running. Even so, I was hoping that I'd proved two things to him. The first was that I had no intention of harming him. The second was that if he chose to leave instead of allowing me to touch his leg, it became a tremendous amount of work for him.

I made every effort to be as quiet and gentle with him as I could when I was touching the leg. In turn, he was allowed to stand and rest. This was a very sharp contrast to the frenzied stampede he was forced into when he chose to leave. I could only hope that he would soon see the difference and decide to stand still because he wanted to, not because he felt he was being forced to.

Happily, by the third day, we had come to an understanding, and I was able to touch all four legs without him even offering to run off. By the fifth day, however, I began to get the feeling that his problem was deeper than I had originally thought.

He would allow me to handle his legs and even pick his feet up off the ground for short periods of time. But something wasn't right. It appeared that having someone pick his feet up caused him physical pain. The reason I say this is that it felt like he was guarding himself each time I lifted a foot, almost as though if the foot got too high, it would hurt him terribly. I continued to work with him for the next week, picking his feet up and putting them down. I worked on picking them up a little higher each day and to the point where there was very little opposition on his part. I felt confident that his troubles were almost over.

Then, one week later, I discovered the source of the problem. I picked up his left front foot, just as I had every day for the last fourteen days. Only this time I did something I'd never done before. I brought the leg slightly out to the side, as a farrier would to put the leg between his knees to trim or shoe him. The horse immediately panicked and blew up, almost going over backwards and taking me with him.

He hit the ground running as hard as he could, and there was a look of sheer terror on his face. It was obvious that he hadn't reacted that way just to do it. There was definitely something wrong. He acted like I'd stabbed him with a knife and that all he could do to protect himself was run away.

It just so happened that a local vet was only a few feet away. She had been working on a horse with a puncture wound in its leg and had just finished up when this horse blew.

"Boy," I heard her say, "you've sure got your hands full there."

"Did you see that?" I asked, as she made her way towards the round pen.

"Yeah," she replied. "He's really something, isn't he?"

"Did he look sore to you?"

"Sore?" She shook her head. "I don't think so. He looks spoiled to me."

"No," I replied. "I think I hurt him somehow."

She turned and began to walk away. "You just keep working with him," she said patronizingly. "He'll come around."

Now I'm not one to disagree with someone just for the sake of disagreeing, especially when that somebody is a doctor who's supposed to know what she's talking about. But this horse wasn't spoiled. He was in pain. I left the round pen, walked over to my truck and pulled out the business card of Dr. Dave Siemens, an equine chiropractor who had been recommended to me by a friend who had used him. I gave Dr. Siemens a call and set up an appointment for him to look at the horse.

To tell the truth, I had never put much stock in chiropractors. The whole concept of what they do just never set right with me. The idea that somebody could remove pain by manipulating your spine seemed too far-fetched to be feasible. It isn't surprising, then, that when I first heard somebody mention the term "equine chiropractor" I was, to say the least, skeptical. Actually, I guess I figured these "doctors" had stumbled upon a scam by which they could drain the pocketbooks of unsuspecting horse owners looking for a sure-fire cure to their horse's ailments.

Surely, I figured, it would be those same horse owners who would be standing in line at the Better Business Bureau complaining about how they'd been taken by the scam and looking for a way to get their money back. Of course, by that time, the equine chiropractor would have loaded his ever-ready gypsy wagon and stolen off into the night, smiling a toothy grin and counting the money he'd made (which he kept in a whiskey barrel inside the wagon).

It would then be up to people like me, who knew better to begin with, to stay behind and comfort the folks who had lost all their money in this cruel but ingenious plot. It would also be up to folks like me to throw in an occasional "I told you so" during the comforting process to remind the victims of how foolish they had been, thus preventing the same tragedy from ever occurring again.

This was the image that I'd carried around with me for years. It was during those same years that the mere mention of the term equine chiropractor would bring a smile to my face, if not a downright outburst of laughter at the absurdity of the thing. This was the mindset I had the day I stood near the round pen and watched as a new horse at the stable was being longed. The horse looked very stiff and uncomfortable as he moved in a trot to his right and even worse as he moved to the left. His lope seemed labored and disjointed as he continuously crossfired in the rear and consistently picked up the wrong lead in the front.

As I walked away, I remember thinking that the horse's future prospects weren't very good unless he learned how to move. And in a horse that moved as badly as he did, teaching him was going to be quite an undertaking. The following weekend I happened to notice the same horse. He was again being longed in the round pen and was moving so fluently that I had to take a second look just to make sure it was, in fact, the horse I had watched the week before.

He moved with great ease from one gait to the next and never once missed picking up the correct lead when asked. The change in him was so complete that I had to ask his owner how he'd accomplished the task. What kind of magical training technique got those types of results in only a week's time?

"I didn't do anything," the owner said, as the horse floated effortlessly around him. "He was just real sore."

"What did you do, drug him?" I asked.

"No," he laughed. "I had my chiropractor work on him."

"Chiropractor! You're kidding."

"No," he replied. "He looks pretty good, doesn't he?"

"He sure does," I said, wiping the egg off my face.

I never in a million years would have suspected that a chiropractor could have gotten that type of result on anything, especially a horse. It was an eye-opening experience for me, and I must admit, I haven't looked at equine chiropractic medicine in the same negative way since. In fact, having learned more about the techniques, I have become a big advocate of it and believe in its results. Of course, it isn't the answer to every soreness problem, but in situations where it's applicable, the changes can be amazing.

With this incident in mind, I called Dr. Siemens, and three days later, the three of us, Dr. Siemens, the horse, and myself, were standing in the round pen. For some reason, when he arrived I'd expected to see my idea of a typical doctor, a tall, thin man with graying hair, soft spoken, serious, and to the point. What I found was quite the opposite.

Dr. Siemens was a very friendly, outgoing, and happy fellow who took the time to ask serious questions and watch how the horse moved while at the same time pulling on his beard and cracking jokes. He wasn't all that tall either, 5 feet 6 inches or so, and he was dressed in jeans and tennis shoes. However, his knowledge of equine anatomy and his understanding of the seriousness of this horse's problem quickly became apparent as he started to press, feel, and pull on certain areas of the horse's body. Within minutes he had pinpointed the areas of this horse's soreness.

"He's sore in both shoulders, hips, and withers," he said. "His neck is a little sore, too, but not as bad. And he's worse on the left side than on the right."

"Well," I asked, "can we fix him?"

"Oh, sure," he replied. "It'll take a few visits, but he should be good as new."

Two weeks later, the horse's owner arrived to see how he was doing. She had been out of town for the past three weeks, so I hadn't been able to tell her what we'd found until that day. I explained how the horse's problem had stemmed from his soreness. Each time a farrier picked a foot up to work on it, it caused him unbearable pain. His natural response was to take the leg back. The farrier, in turn, would again pick up the foot, causing pain. It had gotten to the point where the horse, anticipating that he was going to be hurt, had decided not to let anybody touch his legs. From there the problem had snowballed.

Dr. Siemens' work on the horse had all but eliminated the soreness, which made picking up his feet no longer painful. Of course, we also had to work through the fact that even though it no longer hurt to have his feet picked up, he would still anticipate the pain, which would cause him to take a foot away from time to time.

"But," I told her, "I think he's okay now."

With that, I walked into the round pen where the horse was standing, slowly reached down, and, one by one, picked up each of his feet. I then placed them all between my knees as a farrier would, and slapped them hard several times with the palm of my hand. The horse never even flinched.

I am now a firm believer in chiropractic medicine and have since used Dr. Dave on countless horses. I have found that many problems that we think are stubbornness or the horse being spoiled are actually caused by soreness that simply will not allow the horse to do what we are asking. When you eliminate the soreness, you eliminate the problem.

Of course, soreness isn't the cause one hundred percent of the time, especially when it comes to picking up a horse's foot. You see, most people think that standing on three legs comes natural to a horse, so they don't understand why, when first trying to teach a horse to pick its feet up, the horse often reacts by taking the foot away. And then, why he does it in a mean or belligerent manner.

Well, he does those things for two reasons. First, by picking a foot up, you're taking away his ability to flee. If he can't run away, he can't use his flight instinct. Second, he doesn't know how to stand on three legs. It not only throws his balance off but also forces him to distribute his weight on the remaining three legs that are on the ground. This causes an even bigger problem for him because his body weight is distributed unevenly to begin with, with about sixty percent of it being on his front feet and only forty percent on the back.

I recall the first horse I ever worked with on picking its feet up. It was an eight-month-old filly that had never had her feet worked with before, and I was having a heck of a time with her. Each time I tried to pick a foot up, she'd immediately take it back, fighting and kicking the entire time. I'd been working with her for nearly an hour and hadn't gotten any further than when I started. In fact, it had gotten to the point where she would start to move away from me anytime I got near her leg. I was just getting ready to give up when the old man came over.

"Come here for a minute," he said, gesturing me to follow him. We went over and stopped a short distance from the barn. He turned and looked directly at me.

"Turn around," he said bluntly. "I need to see something."

"What?" I asked.

"Turn around," he repeated. "I need to see something." This is weird, I thought, as I turned around.

"Okay, now bend your left leg backwards." Puzzled, I turned and looked back at him.

"Don't look at me," he grunted. "Just do it."

I faced the other way and slowly bent my left leg backwards at the knee. I had no sooner raised it a short distance than he reached down and grabbed my leg at the ankle.

"What are you doing?" I asked, fighting to get my balance.

"Hold on for a second," he replied. "I need to see something."

He then began to move my leg back and forth, up and down, and finished by slapping the sole of my boot with his hand. I lost my balance completely and had begun to fall forward when he finally let go.

"What the hell was that all about?" I shouted, regaining my balance.

"I thought your heel was loose," he said, matter-of-factly. "I guess it wasn't." With that he turned and walked into the barn.

I shook my head at his strange behavior, turned, and walked back over to the filly. I reached down, grabbed ahold of her ankle, and was getting ready to pull it upward when the idea of what had just occurred hit me.

The old man didn't want to look at the heel of my boot, he wanted to show me how it felt to have a leg pulled and jerked on. He wanted me to see what it was like to be pulled off balance and not understand why, and he wanted me to stop doing the same thing to that filly. It was a lesson well learned and one that has stuck with me all these years.

Most of the horses I've seen that have trouble picking up their feet have all been trained in the same way. The person doing the training did so by insisting the horse hold the foot up, even though the horse didn't understand what the person was asking. As a result, the horse was inadvertently taught to fight whenever someone tried to lift a foot off the ground.

I have found that this problem can be avoided by breaking the whole process into very short and distinct steps and by not expecting too much from the horse at one time. With most horses, colts included, I simply start by getting the animal used to having its legs handled. This means petting and stroking them from shoulder to hoof in the front and hip to hoof in the rear.

Once I can do that, I'll place my hand lightly on the cannon bone and gently lean into the horse, taking his weight off that particular foot. From there I ask him to pick the foot up, only an inch or so at a time, until he willingly picks the foot up as high as I need it to be. I also make sure I can bring the foot forward to put it in the position it needs to be when placed on a hoof stand, and off to the side so that it can be placed between my knees. The key to being successful is to go slow, no faster than the horse can, and take the time to work through trouble spots. Nine times out of ten, the horse will respond favorably within a day or two and never be a problem. However, it's that one horse out of the ten that you have to worry about.

He then began to move my leg back and forth, up and down.

Usually if a horse isn't responding, it's because he can't, due to soreness somewhere. Every once in a great while, though, you get one that doesn't want to conform because he simply wants to be contrary. The worst horse I ever worked with that had that problem was a two-year-old gelding named Thunder.

I had worked with Thunder for nearly seven months. Of those months, three were spent working specifically on his feet. He was a very independent and cranky sort that would have been quite content had he never seen a human being during his lifetime. To him, humans were nothing but a constant source of aggravation and stress that he would not tolerate, and conforming to anything we asked of him was simply out of the question. He was so bad that, in the beginning, he wouldn't even allow himself to be petted. This is an extremely unusual attitude for a horse to have, and frankly I haven't seen it in very many.

In his defense, I must say he was probably that way due to an incident that occurred when he was a baby. Both he and his mother had been caught in a stampede of sorts, and he was knocked down and run over by several horses. As a result, he had become very anti-social, so much so that he would not feed or lie down when other horses were present and would often be very brazen and standoffish. I believe that it was this same wariness and a strong need for self-preservation that also forced him to act that way towards humans.

It had taken two weeks to get him halter broke and leading. It took a month to get him to quietly accept being saddled and still another month before we were able to get on him. Even that, however, was nothing compared to the trouble we were to have while working with his feet. I remember telling Joy Mathews, one of my students at the time, that he was by far the worst I'd ever seen.

I could see that we were going to have trouble right from the start. Even the worst horses usually decide within a day or two that what we're doing isn't that bad, but Thunder simply had no ambition to work with us. It was three weeks before we could even touch all four legs, and another month before we could pick up all four feet. Even then, we were only able to pick them up. If we tried to clean the foot or move it in any way, he would completely blow the cork. He'd violently pull his foot away and stampede off, perfectly content to run for as long as he could, circling countless times inside the round pen.

It had gotten to the point where he actually preferred running to standing still and allowing his legs to be touched. We also found that he would stand tied, but if we tried to do anything with his feet, he'd simply kick us. Even though having him loose while working with him meant he'd simply run around and not allow himself to be handled, I decided that it was better than the alternative, being kicked.

The trouble was, we weren't getting much done with him because he'd spend all of his time running and little, if any time, being worked. We needed to find a way to make running miserable for him. We had to make it so much work that he no longer wanted to use it as an option.

I decided the best way to do that was to restrict the movement of one of his legs. Not restrict it to the point where he couldn't use the leg at all, but rather to where there was enough tension on it that using it became extremely difficult.

I went to the truck and brought back one of the thirty-foot cotton driving lines that I'd made years before. A metal snap was braided into one end of the rope, and a small loop was braided in the other end. The loop was just big enough so that the other end of the rope could be brought through and would slide freely, creating a collapsible loop similar to a lariat loop.

Having made a loop with the rope, I laid it on the ground inside the pen. Joy led Thunder over the loop, and when he placed his left hind foot in the middle, I pulled the slack, catching the foot.

As soon as his foot was caught, Joy let go of the lead rope, and the rodeo was on. As Joy made her way out of the pen, I took up my position in the pen's center, and Thunder ran furiously around me. He was running as fast as he could, while bucking at the same time. He was doing everything he could to get the little cotton rope off from around his pastern.

In the meantime, I applied just enough pressure to the rope to cause it to be a major irritant. This meant simply that every time he brought his leg forward, I was applying pressure to the rope, which caused him to feel a dragging sensation. At the same time, he would occasionally step on the lead rope that was attached to the halter and dragging on the ground, which caused him to pull his own head down. Between having his head pulled down in the front and having to drag a hind foot each time he moved, he soon figured out that running away wasn't near as much fun as it had been in the past.

Even with that, it still took nearly four days before he decided on his own that running was no longer the correct choice. Having finally shown him that the easy thing to do in this situation was to stand still, we quickly came upon another obstacle.

As I said before, by this time he would allow us to pick his feet up, but if we asked anything else from him, such as cleaning the hoof or moving the leg in any other way, he would defiantly take the foot away, then step a few paces to the side. He did this with such speed and agility that we simply couldn't hold him. As a result, we weren't getting anything done, and he was getting into a very bad habit, taking his foot away whenever he pleased.

Again, we needed to remove that option. I decided to do that by not allowing him to have the leg. The technique that I was forced to use was an absolute last resort and is not one that I relish using or recommend, because if done wrong, it can cause serious injury to the horse.

What I did was bring out my seldom-used one-inch cotton rope. It's about twelve feet long with a loop braided in one end, just like the cotton longe line. In this case, I made a

I applied just enough pressure to the rope to cause it to be a major irritant.

small loop with the rope and put it around the pastern of a front foot. I then took the rest of the rope and put it over his back so the end of it came down on his other side. I gently lifted the foot and held it in the position that he was comfortable with, while at the same time tying the other end of the rope around the same pastern.

I took out a hoof pick and began cleaning the hoof. As expected, he tried to take the foot away, only to find that he couldn't. He didn't like that very much and immediately blew the cork. He reared up, going over backwards, floundered around on the ground for a bit, and finally made it back to his feet (at least the three he could still get on the ground). He then began to run as best he could around the pen, going only about twenty feet before stopping.

I let him stand by himself for a short time before approaching, petting him, and letting the leg down. We went back to the middle of the pen, then started all over. By the end of an hour's time, we no longer needed the rope to pick that foot up, clean it, or move it around in any position. However, the next day, we had to start all over again with that foot and, in the weeks that followed, had to use the same technique on each of the other three legs as well.

After about a month's time, he had finally gotten to the point where we no longer needed ropes to help him pick his feet up. We could pick them up and clean them out, and at one point, I even trimmed them. But still, I always got the feeling that he was doing it under protest, and that at any time, he was going to blow.

In a way, I really admired Thunder. He wasn't being contrary because of soreness or because he didn't understand what we wanted or even because he was mean or rank. He was doing it because he simply didn't want to conform. He saw absolutely no reason why he, a horse, should have to fit into a human's world and fought the idea of it every inch of the way. Only after we had given him no other choice did he finally do what we asked.

In all the time that I had worked with Thunder, he never changed. He stuck to his principles and ideals and would do what was asked only if he had to. We worked with him every day in a constant and consistent manner, trying to show him the way things were to be from now on. Day after day he would do the things that were asked, but always under protest.

Suddenly, one day, his attitude changed. It happened literally overnight. He had gone from a cantankerous, rebellious individual to a broke horse. It was as if he finally had conceded to us. It was as if he was saying, "Hey, I can't beat you, so I might as well join you."

All of our hard work and persistence had paid off. The horse had finally submitted and would, from now on, be a good boy. I must admit, though, for me it was a hollow victory. Watching him stand passively while his owner walked around him, picking up one foot after another, I couldn't help but get the feeling that we had broke this horse in the true sense of the word. We had broken his spirit.

Horses like Thunder are more the exception than the rule and are few and far between, especially when it comes to working with their feet. He did prove one thing though. Even with horses like him, the job can be accomplished by being quiet, consistent, and patient.

Most horses want to learn and do what is asked. They simply want to be asked in a way they can understand. It's just that most people see working with horse's feet as an unpleasant and dangerous task and want to get it done as quickly as possible. The problem with that is just because you do it quickly doesn't mean it's done right. The thing to remember here is, if you don't have the time to do it right, you will have to take the time to do it over. And nobody wants to do that, especially the horse.

NOTES FOR PICKING UP FEET

The main difference between what I do today when picking up a horse's foot and what I did back when I wrote this chapter is actually relatively subtle and has more to do with an overall shift of attitude throughout my horsemanship, and my life, over the years than it does a change of technique. The shift of attitude I'm talking about has to do with looking for more peaceful and quiet solutions to problems than anything else, which I believe has helped temper my approach to most—if not all—horse related situations.

I must say that along with that shift, some of the things I do to help a horse pick up their feet have changed, too. For instance, I seldom work a horse loose in a pen and then move them around if they don't want to stand still anymore. I also don't use a footrope much anymore, although there are still times when it does seem prudent to do so.

These days, instead of going right to trying to pick up the foot of a horse that obviously has problems, I always check for any physical issues the horse might have first, such as soreness or stiffness in a hip, hock, stifle, shoulder, knee, etc. In doing so I have found that more times than not an old or nagging injury of some sort is the cause of the trouble in the first place. Often by treating the injury appropriately, the problem either goes away completely or gets much easier to work with over all.

This was also the chapter in which I introduce for the first time my longtime friend and chiropractor, Dr. Dave Siemens. Dr. Dave is by far one of the finest equine chiropractors I have ever had the opportunity to work with, and since this book first came out the two of us have worked on thousands of horses together all over the world. I have learned much of what I know about equine anatomy, joint function, and gait analysis from him, and it was because of him that I now look for pain and/or soreness issues first whenever I am dealing with any kind of problem behavior a horse is exhibiting.

Headshyness

A certain day comes to mind whenever I think of all I've learned about working with headshy horses. It was one of those days when I would've been better off never climbing out of bed. I started that day with a flat tire. It was nearly impossible to get the lug nuts off due to the force of the impact wrench used to put them on at the tire shop, but with brute strength and persistence, I managed to get the tire changed in forty-five minutes, making me nearly an hour late for my first appointment.

I'd promised to help a friend, Lloyd, round up his herd of horses so they could be wormed, vaccinated, and have their feet trimmed. By the time I arrived, the horses had already been brought in and were milling around in the large catch pen. The farrier had been there for nearly forty-five minutes and had already finished five head. After apologizing for my tardiness and enduring several good-humored pokes at my apparent inability to get there on time, I gathered up a few halters and entered the pen.

The system was very simple. I would go in and catch the horses, two at a time, and bring them out of the pen to the back of Lloyd's pickup where he would vaccinate and worm them. I then took them over and tied them to a long hitch rail where they would stand until the farrier was ready for them.

I had just finished tying up the first two horses and had gone back into the pen to catch two more. As I was walking past the back end of a gray mare named Lacey, she suddenly let out a warning kick aimed at a nearby gelding. It was just my luck that day that I happened to be passing between the two when she kicked, and the blow meant for the gelding hit me squarely on the left cheek of my butt. The force of the kick literally picked me up off the ground and dumped me about four feet away.

"Watch out for Lacey," I heard Lloyd call. "She's in heat and a little cranky."

"Thanks for the warning," I grunted, picking myself up off the ground and rubbing my bruised behind. I should have known the kind of day it was going to be right then and cashed it in, but I had another appointment. Before too long, we had caught, wormed, and vaccinated all the horses in the pen, and with nothing left to do but trim them, it was time for me to go.

My next stop was to look at a horse that one of my customers was thinking about purchasing. I pulled up to the house where the horse was being kept, and because I was running late, both my customer and the horse's owner were waiting.

After again apologizing for my tardiness, we began to give the horse the once over. He was about 15.2 hands, bay, and heavily muscled. His owner went on and on about all the things this horse could do. "He was broke to ride or drive," he said. You could also rope off him, run barrels, hunt, pack, or do any kind of trail riding. In other words, the horse was virtually bombproof.

"Well," I said, after listening to the horse's long list of virtues, "could you throw a saddle on him so we can see him work?"

"You bet," the gentleman said cheerfully. He went into the barn and returned with a heavy roping saddle. He quickly groomed the horse, then put the saddle pad and saddle on the horse's back.

While the horse was being saddled, I stood on the other side of the hitch rail, about two feet away from the horse's head. My attention was split between listening to my client's chatter about the unseasonably warm weather and watching the way the horse's owner was cinching the horse. He had slowly reached under the horse and gotten ahold of the cinch. Then, equally as slowly, he brought the cinch up and put it in position to be tightened.

As he slid the latigo through the cinch ring, I noticed the horse's head begin to raise, a sign that he was becoming concerned. The man looped the latigo back up through the saddle rigging, down again through the cinch ring, and began ever so slowly to tighten the cinch. I could see that the tighter he got the cinch, the more concerned the horse was becoming.

"Is this horse a little cinchy?" I asked.

"A little," he replied, still drawing the cinch tight.

Without warning, the horse turned at me with fire in his eyes, laid his ears back, and bit me soundly on the shoulder. With almost the same speed and intensity, the man immediately reached over and, with a closed fist, whacked the horse squarely in the mouth.

As I pedaled backwards trying to get away from the attacking horse, the horse did the same, trying to get away from the attacking man. The horse hit the end of his lead rope with such force that the rope broke, sending the horse falling over backwards. He quickly scrambled to his feet and took off running. The saddle, which the man hadn't been able to get completely tight, soon slipped to the horse's side and then to his belly. It wasn't long before the horse was running down the road, bucking and kicking at the saddle that was now hanging under him, while his owner sprinted behind waving his arms and yelling obscenities.

The horse had bitten me with such force that I could feel the muscle in my shoulder start to swell. My client rushed over and sympathetically asked if I was all right. I told her I was, even though the arm already hurt from my shoulder clear down past my elbow.

"How come he bit you like that?" she asked, as we watched the horse, by now about a quarter mile away, finally kick the saddle loose.

"Because I was closest," I told her. "He probably would have bit anybody or anything that happened to be in front of him. This time it just happened to be me."

I explained to her that in some severe cases of horses being cinchy (not wanting to be cinched up), they feel an overwhelming need to defend themselves. Because I was directly in his line of sight, I was the one he was defending himself from. So, naturally, I was the one that got bit.

"Can that problem be fixed?" she asked, watching as the horse disappeared over the next hill.

"It can," I told her, "but if it were me, I think I'd look for a horse that was a little more solid. There are too many good horses out there for you to want to buy something like that."

A short time later I found myself back in my truck and heading for my next appointment. The aggressiveness of the horse that bit me, along with the other misfortunes of the day, would combine to change the way I worked with horses, but it was hard to see anything positive about the day right then.

The rope broke, sending the horse falling over backwards.

The horse I was to see next was being boarded at a stable about ten miles south of Denver. Luckily, I was traveling on the interstate during non-rush hours, so I figured that I'd finally be able to get to an appointment on time.

Of course, I should have known better. Driving south, I soon found myself stuck in a traffic jam nearly two miles long because of a tractor-trailer rig that had jackknifed, blocking three of the four lanes of the interstate. Waiting for traffic to start flowing again, I sat trying to relieve the pressure of my aching butt by lifting it off the seat, while at the same time trying to avoid leaning on the door with my swollen shoulder.

This time I was only an hour and a half late getting to the stable where the horse was being kept. After another sincere and heartfelt apology for being late, I was ushered into the barn to see the horse. He was a big, sorrel quarter horse gelding that had a very severe head tossing problem. Anytime you got your hand anywhere near his ears, he would violently throw his head in an effort to get away from you. Surprisingly, though, he would allow himself to be haltered. You could even put a bridle on him, providing you took the bridle apart so that it didn't have to be slipped on over his ears.

Now, a horse usually becomes headshy for one of two reasons, either mishandling or lack of handling. In either case, however, the results are usually the same. The horse becomes hard to halter, bridle, touch around the head area, and sometimes even hard to catch. The owner had become so upset with the head tossing and the danger that was involved in simply touching the horse's ears, that he'd decided finally to try to have the problem fixed.

As we approached the horse, he was standing quietly tied in the aisle of the barn. I untied the horse and began to pet him gently on his shoulder. He appeared quite content and happy to allow me to do that and showed no real sign of concern as I moved farther up his neck, petting him closer to his head.

Seeing that these areas were really of no concern, I slowly continued upward towards his ear. By the time I reached his cheek, I could see the fear beginning to grow in his eyes. Knowing that this was starting to be a problem, I decided to spend a little time in that area showing him that my hand being there wasn't going to cause him any harm.

By keeping my hand on his cheek and softly petting him there, his fear soon diminished. I then moved my hand back to his neck and shoulder before returning to his cheek. After about fifteen minutes he had become just as relaxed with my hand on his cheek as he was with it on his shoulder.

When I felt confident that having my hand on his cheek no longer presented a problem for him, I once again began slowly to advance it towards his ear. This time it didn't take long to find out where his real problem area was. As my finger tips got within about three inches of his ear, he suddenly jerked his head away. He did it with such speed that I had absolutely no time to react.

Up to this point, I'd been holding onto his lead rope with my left hand, while doing all the petting with my right. I decided that instead of holding on to the lead rope, I might be better off holding directly on to the halter. That way, when he went to jerk his head away, I would have a little better hold, making it harder for him to get away from the pressure that my right hand was apparently causing him to feel.

At this point I explained to the horse's owner that each time someone had tried to touch this horse's ears, he had been able to stop them by simply jerking his head away. In a sense, what he had done was actually teach people to leave his ears alone. What we needed to do was not allow him to get away from us. That way we would be able to show him that even though he jerked his head away, he wouldn't get away from the pressure. Once he understood that he couldn't get away, he'd stop fighting. Then we could begin to work on finding the cause of the problem and, in turn, fix it.

Now this is a very common and widely used method of working with headshy horses and is a technique that I had used variations of on countless occasions. I had found that most horses conform to the idea in a relatively short period of time, usually within an hour or so. I felt confident that this horse would be no different. Unfortunately, no one had told that to the horse.

I began working with him again, starting at his shoulder and slowly moving my hand back up towards his head. Again, there was no sign of concern until I reached the area near his ear. He quickly jerked his head up, but because I was now holding the halter with my left hand, I was able to hold him good enough to keep my right hand in position near his ear. He responded by quickly jerking his head to the right, away from me, two more times. Still, I was able to keep my hand in position.

Suddenly, and unexpectedly, he threw his head directly at me, hitting me squarely on the end of my nose. He hit me with such force that it knocked me to my knees and sent my hat ten feet down the aisle. Luckily, the halter that he was wearing was tight enough that my hand remained stuck between it and his face, so I hadn't lost my grip on him.

He then jumped to the right, away from me, pulling me right off the ground, and went into a spin right there in the middle of the aisle. By this time, however, I'd managed to reach up with my right hand and get ahold of his mane. He continued to spin and I continued to hold on, my feet touching the ground only periodically. After about six full revolutions, during which time he stepped on my foot once and managed to hit my left knee on a stall door twice, he finally came to a stop.

The good news was that he had just made his best effort at trying to get rid of me and had been unsuccessful. The bad news was that I now had a bloody nose, a stepped-on foot, and a banged-up knee. These things seemed to fit right in with my already sore shoulder and bruised butt.

After taking about five minutes to rest, recuperate, and allow the horse to settle down, we started all over again. This time, I slowed my actions down considerably. Each time the horse began to show signs of concern I backed off that area for a short period before continuing on. In this way, I was showing him that I wasn't going to dwell on an area that was a problem spot but, rather, try to slowly work through it with him. This was a very tedious process and after about forty-five minutes, I had only managed to get about an inch closer to the ear than when we started.

Obviously, we hadn't been working the entire time either. During any training session, it's extremely important to give the horse a break from what you're doing. This allows him to relax and clear his head and also allows for what you're doing to sink in. In this case, I would occasionally stop what I was doing and walk him around for a few minutes. I also took him over and allowed him to drink a couple of times, and once I simply tied him up and let him stand for a while.

By the same token, I made every effort when I was working with him to be as consistent and constant as I possibly could. This meant that I tried to reward him for proper behavior by relieving the pressure I'd been applying. Usually this simply meant that I'd remove my hand from the problem area. If he attempted to jerk his head away, I made every effort to keep my hand in the spot that seemed to cause the reaction.

By working in this slow and painstaking manner, I was finally able to work my way up the horse's ears. It had taken nearly two-and-a-half hours to do it, though, and during that time the horse was obviously under a lot of stress and had blown up several more times.

By the time I finally left, I was able not only to touch both of his ears, but also bend them forwards, backwards, and to the sides. I could also slip his bridle over his ears without having to take it apart. I could even gently put my fingers inside his ears.

I explained to the horse's owner that what he might want to do for the next month or so was handle the horse's ears every time he came in contact with him. Make it so much a part of the horse's handling, I told the owner, that it simply becomes second nature to him, and before long he will forget all about having the problem.

As I sat caught in Denver's afternoon rush-hour traffic while trying to make my way home, a couple of things were going through my mind concerning the horse I'd just worked with. The first was that the entire time that I worked with him, I had him restrained. In a

He then jumped to the right, pulling me right off the ground.

sense I had limited his most basic instinct of survival, the ability to flee. The second was that his problem was severe enough that he had considered my movement towards his ears as aggression. In response, he tried to do what comes natural. He tried to get away. I got to thinking that even though he threw me around some, I was lucky that he hadn't resorted to aggression himself by rearing, striking, or biting. It was that concern, made stronger by the day I was having, along with the obvious stress that I had put him through, that caused me to rethink the method I'd used on him and others like him.

I began wondering about the possibilities of working with a headshy horse using no restraint whatsoever, no lead rope or halter. I thought that by working with him in such a way it might limit his stress by allowing him to get completely away from the situation if things got too scary. With his flight instinct intact, I felt that this would also eliminate the possibility of him becoming violent or aggressive towards me.

The one thing that worried me about this idea was the possibility of the horse running away and not wanting to come back. If that happened, I felt I would be reinforcing that response, making the technique unusable. For that reason I thought it would be imperative for the horse to have complete trust in me before trying this approach. Hopefully, he would feel that even though I was trying to touch a spot that was sensitive enough to make him want to run away, he would think I was safe enough to want to return to. If he returned of his own free will, I felt it would show an effort to continue on his part. It would then be up to me to keep this positive momentum going.

My biggest concern was that I'd never seen or heard of anybody trying this before. As a result, I had no firsthand information, good or bad, to go on. It was that uncertainty about the outcome that kept me from trying the idea for a long time. Then, some months later, I received two horses that were severely headshy. The first was a two-year-old half-Arab filly, the other a twelve-year-old registered Arab mare. Both had been abused in the past and were extremely difficult to halter. The filly was so bad that her owner had left her halter on for over a year. He was afraid that if he took it off, he wouldn't be able to get it back on. To make matters worse, she seemed deathly afraid of people and was very aggressive. The older mare, while also having a fear of people, was less aggressive. She would, however, fight violently to get away any time you moved a hand to the vicinity of her head, especially her ears.

Because both animals' problems were so severe, I decided to try the restraint-free technique that I'd wondered about while driving back from Denver that day. I was fairly confident that even if the technique didn't work, there wasn't much chance of making them any worse than they already were. With that in mind, I brought the filly out and turned her loose in our fifty-foot round pen.

I took her halter off and, as expected, she spun and headed directly to the rail. I took up my position in the center of the pen as she ran in circles around me. Occasionally she would throw a glance in my direction and snort threateningly. After about five minutes, obviously feeling threatened by my presence, she suddenly turned in my direction and charged. This was not your average halfhearted charge, but a full-blown, ears-back charge, front feet high and striking.

In the past, if a horse charged me, my reaction was simple. I swung my lead rope in his direction, sometimes striking him with it if he got too close. In a sense, I was meeting aggression with aggression. Only a few days earlier, however, I had witnessed something that made me reconsider even this simple technique.

While filling water tanks, I'd noticed a stray cat wandering across our property. My dog Sadie, a playful springer spaniel, black lab mix, also noticed the cat and bounced over to investigate. As Sadie got closer, the cat began to hunch up, making itself look bigger. The closer Sadie got, the bigger the cat got, until finally Sadie stopped approaching. They stood looking at one another for a couple of minutes before Sadie turned and bounced away. The cat had saved itself from a confrontation by simply making itself look bigger.

Remembering this, I tried to make myself "bigger" as the filly charged by raising my arms. My reason for doing this instead of swinging my lead rope was to try to show the horse that I was not there for a confrontation and, at the same time, to try to lessen what she might consider an aggressive posture on my part.

Surprisingly enough, the filly veered off almost immediately, headed back to the rail, spun, and stopped. As she did this, I stepped back a few paces to further lessen the pressure that she had been feeling. This seemed to set the stage for the remainder of our session.

From then on, each time the filly responded favorably, either by facing me, standing still, or approaching, I tried to relieve the pressure she was feeling by backing away. Each time she moved away from me, I would put the pressure on by following her and lightly kicking dirt in her direction. She soon found that she could become more comfortable by being next to me.

Within about forty-five minutes, she had settled down completely. No longer aggressive, she approached quietly and would follow willingly. In less than an hour, I felt confident enough to begin working on her headshyness. I began by touching, petting, and stroking her in the shoulder area. I then widened the area to include her neck, back, sides, and front legs, being careful to watch her reactions for possible problem areas. As I moved my attention closer to her head, she became slightly concerned. When that would happen,

I immediately returned to her shoulder, then slowly worked my way back up. Each time, I stopped as soon as she got nervous. In the process, however, I found I wasn't getting much closer to my destination, her ears and the poll area between them.

After about thirty minutes, it became apparent that in order to see if the technique was going to work, I needed to cross the imaginary boundary that the filly had put up. The line seemed to be about three inches from her ear, and I received an immediate reaction as I crossed it. She jerked her head away from my hand, snorted, and ran off. She circled the pen twice, then turned and faced me. As before, I backed up a few steps, which was enough to draw her back to me. When I felt she'd settled down sufficiently, I began the process over.

She ran off each time I breached the line after that but always returned. After about a half dozen tries, she was returning so willingly that I decided to begin putting some pressure on her as she moved away. I would, thereby, be making it more work for her to move away than it was to stay.

The next time she ran off, I clapped my hands and kicked a little dirt in her direction. She became noticeably concerned but once again returned to allow me to try again. We repeated this several times. Within about twenty minutes, I was able to work my hand up so that it rested between her ears. Once she allowed me to touch her there, I found it increasingly easier to take my hand away and put it back with little or no resistance on her part. I decided then that it would be enough for one day. The following day, we were able to get to that point in less than fifteen minutes. We were still having a problem with her ears, however. Each time I tried to touch them, she would immediately panic and run off.

The breakthrough here actually came by accident. As I was resting my hand on her poll, something behind her got her attention. She turned her ears back and tipped them down slightly to hear what the noise was. By doing this, she accidentally laid her ears on my hand. I noticed that as long as she was touching me, she wasn't concerned, but if I made the effort to touch her, she would become frightened and run off. Realizing this, I began to place my hand in positions behind her ears so that when she moved her ears back she would touch me. I would then ever so slightly move my fingers in order to touch her in return. By using this slow and easy method, she was soon allowing me to handle her ears freely.

By the third day, you wouldn't have known that the filly ever had a headshy problem. She was quiet and very content to let me handle her in areas that would have been unthinkable only seventy-two hours earlier. As happy as I was with the results of this technique on the filly, I was even more impressed with the way the older mare reacted to it. Following basically the same steps, the twelve-year-old was letting me handle her ears in less than an hour.

I have since used that simple restraint-free technique on horses with bridling and other handling problems. In each case, the animal has responded quickly, usually within fifteen to forty-five minutes, depending on the type and severity of the problem. I should point out that in some of the cases, the technique did need to be reinforced the following day, always with positive results.

The thing that I like most about the method is the genuine lack of desire of the horses to fight. I have now used it on more horses than I care to remember, and in each case, when the pressure became too great, the horse would simply leave. The interesting thing is that they all returned of their own free will or would allow me to approach them. It's almost as if they want to work on their problems as long as they can do it at their pace.

I also feel I have more control over the loose horse than I do over the restrained one. The reason for this is that when working with the restrained horse, I feel I am, in a sense, forcing myself and my ideas upon him. The restrained horse often reacts in fear and a fearful horse, unable to flee, can be unpredictable. Knowing that the frightened horse is unpredictable causes me concern. So even though I might think I'm in control of the situation, deep down I know I'm not.

On the other hand, we know that if something scares the unrestrained horse, he will run away. With his first instinct of survival still intact, he slowly begins to gain confidence both in us and in the situation. By letting the horse get away but then putting pressure on him to leave, we are giving him the opportunity to figure out which is harder, going away or staying. The horse then feels that he has some control over what happens. What we are doing is helping him make his decision, which ultimately puts us in the leadership role and in control of the situation.

It's funny how on that day months earlier, arriving home four hours late, broken, bruised, and sore literally from my head to my toes, all I could think of was what a lousy day I'd had. It wasn't until some time later that it finally occurred to me how good a day it actually had been.

Had it not been for all the stress and aggravation that I'd gone through, I may have never given a second thought to the technique I'd used when working with that headshy horse in Denver. However, because of everything that happened that day, I began to make an effort to find a technique that was easier on both the horses with similar problems and myself. As it turns out, I found that I'd learned more from that one lousy day than I had from most of my good days combined. What they say is true. Behind every dark cloud, there's a silver lining. I guess sometimes you just have to wait for the storm to be over before you can see it.

NOTES FOR HEADSHYNESS

As with the chapter on picking up feet, the changes in the way I work with headshy horses have more to do with an overall attitude shift than a change of technique. Although I must admit I am much less apt to "insist" that a headshy horse's head stay in one place while I work with them, as I described toward the beginning of the chapter. These days I will move with the horse using the least amount of pressure possible to do so, while still giving the horse some guidance. I have found this to be a much more quiet and effective way of working with the horse.

Trailer loading

The very hot, dry, and dusty day had been made even worse by the fact that I'd been standing all morning and afternoon in a shadeless riding arena giving a trailer-loading demonstration. Despite the nearly ninety-five-degree heat, which seemed even more intense as I stood on the sandy floor of the arena, the clinic had actually gone quite well. Even so, I was happy to be on my way to the coolness of the little mountain town of Estes Park where I make my home.

It wasn't until the long line of summer tourist traffic I'd been stuck in reached town that I remembered I had to pick up my mail. Because there's little mail delivery in Estes Park, most residents, including myself, have to go to the post office for our mail.

During the off-season winter months, the post office parking lot is a very easy place to get in to and out of. In the summer, it's a place of unlimited stress and aggravation, with long lines of stalled traffic and seldom, if ever, a place to park.

That's why, on this day, I felt quite lucky to find a parking spot almost immediately. As I returned to my truck after getting the mail, I began to think that as long as I'd been lucky enough to find this parking spot, I might as well get some use out of it. Up to this point, I'd either been stuck in slow-moving traffic or working in the stifling heat of the day. I was hot, dirty, and thirsty, and standing there watching the traffic in the lot move along at a snail's pace, I decided that what might go good right about then was a cold beer.

I threw the mail on the seat of the truck, locked the door, and headed to a nearby watering hole known as the Wheel Bar. The Wheel is a quiet little saloon with a stained oak floor. It's a place where many of the town's local folks go to have a few drinks and discuss the world's problems. I no sooner got in the door than the bartender, a big friendly Texan named Marlin Flowers, poured a beer for me and set it down at an empty spot at the bar.

"How are you today?" he asked, picking up the change left on the bar by the stool's previous occupant.

"Good, Marlin," I replied. "How's the day treating you?"

"Like a redheaded stepchild," he smiled, throwing the change into his tip jar.

"Whatcha been up to Mark?" I heard a voice on my left ask.

The voice belonged to Larry Kitchen. "Kitch," as he's referred to by nearly everyone who knows him, is an ex-bareback bronc rider. He was also a top hand and had worked around horses most of his life, although in recent years, he had kind of gotten away from that line of work.

"I was doing some trailer loading down near Denver," I told him.

"I don't envy you," he said. "I bet it was hotter than a two-dollar pistol down there."

"It sure was," I replied.

"Did you have any trouble?" he asked.

"No," I said, taking a sip from my glass. "They all went in pretty well."

"Boy, I remember one time," he started, "old Harold Bingham was trying to load that big gelding of his in the stock rack of his pickup. He had a ramp for him and everything, and the horse still wouldn't load. He worked on him for a long time before he finally got a lariat and tied it to the horse's halter. Then he ran it up through the stock rack and tied it to the bumper of another pickup.

"He went over to the truck, got his hot shot, and stood behind the horse. On the count of three, he stuck that old horse in the backside with the hot shot, and at the same time the fellow in the pickup took off as fast as he could. Needless to say, they got the horse loaded."

"I bet they did," I said. "Did it cure him from being hard to load?"

"Cure him," Kitch laughed. "Hell, it ruined him. After that you couldn't go anywhere near the back of any kind of truck or trailer without that horse trying to jump in. It didn't matter if it was a pickup, furniture truck, delivery wagon, or whatever. By God, that horse was going to load and load right now. He didn't even care if someone was on his back." Kitch paused for a second, taking the last sip of his beer. "Yes sir, by golly, they sure ruined that horse."

"Ruining them is easy," I added. "It's fixing them that's the hard part."

"Boy, isn't that the truth," he said, signaling Marlin to fill his now empty glass. "I worked for a guy that used to say you can sweet talk a horse into just about anything, but you can't force 'em into nothin', especially getting into a trailer. If you do, that horse will give you nothin' but grief for the rest of his days."

As far as I was concerned, there was never a more accurate statement. Unfortunately, it's not one that is believed by very many people. It has been my experience, specifically concerning trailer loading, that if the horse doesn't load within the first ten or fifteen minutes of trying, the person loses first his patience and then his temper.

The other thing I've noticed about trailer loading is that nearly everybody thinks they're an expert at doing it, whether they are or not. I have never seen it fail. The minute it appears that somebody is having trouble getting his or her horse into a trailer, people, often perfect strangers who know neither the horse nor the horse's owner, appear out of nowhere to offer assistance. Nine times out of ten they do nothing more than make matters worse.

I recall one time I'd been asked by a woman, who was moving her horse from one boarding stable to another, to help her get the horse loaded. Her husband and three or four of his friends had tried to muscle him in a couple of days earlier, but after two-and-a-half hours, they had finally given up. Upon arriving at the place, I found the horse, a small, bay foxtrotter, tied to the two-horse trailer that we were to use. The woman was standing nearby, and there was virtually no one else in sight.

It has been my observation that horses that have trouble loading generally do so for one of three reasons. The first is that they're afraid of the trailer. More specifically, they're afraid of the threat of total confinement that a trailer, especially a two-horse trailer, poses.

Second, they may refuse to load simply because at some point in the past, they balked at loading, and the owner was unable to find a way to motivate them to get in. As a result, they may be a little spoiled.

The third reason is that they're afraid of what will happen to them as they approach the trailer. In other words, each time they get anywhere near the trailer door, somebody has always beat on them to try to force them to get in. Now, this type of horse isn't afraid to get in the trailer. What they are afraid of is getting near the trailer. It just makes sense that if they're afraid to get near the trailer, they aren't going to be able to get in. After working with the little fox trotter for only a few minutes, it became clear that this was his problem. He was afraid to approach the trailer.

The good news is that with this type of horse, getting them to load is usually not very hard. It's simply a matter of quietly gaining their trust while at the same time rewarding them for any offer they make to get closer to the trailer.

The fox trotter's fear was evident as I slowly brought him near the back of the trailer. His body was rigid, his eyes were open wide, and he halfheartedly attempted to rear and back away a couple of times. Each time he tried to back up, I would allow him to go as far as he liked. When he stopped, I'd let him stand quietly for a few minutes, then begin to bring him back towards the trailer. At no point did I try to force him forward, but rather I tried to gently coax him. I did this by applying light pressure on the lead rope. Each time he offered any forward movement, even if it was a shift of his weight, I released the pressure.

Within ten minutes, the horse was quietly standing with his head inside the trailer and his front feet just outside the door. I let him stand like this for a few minutes without asking him to step in. Then, to relieve some of the pressure that he'd obviously been feeling, I took him completely away from the trailer. This not only relieves the pressure, but also gives the horse time to think about what we're doing, without the threat of the trailer looming in front of him.

After standing some distance away from the trailer, we turned and slowly made our way back. He approached the door without hesitation and again stood with his head inside the right-hand compartment with his front feet just outside. We repeated this whole process three more times. Each of those times, I also climbed into the left-side compartment of the trailer. This is where I would be when I asked him to step in for the first time so I wanted him to be used to seeing me there.

When I was confident that he was completely comfortable approaching and standing at the door, I finally began to ask him to step in. I did this, again, by applying light pressure on the lead rope and releasing any time he offered any forward movement. Almost immediately, the horse began to show his willingness to cooperate by lifting and setting down first one front foot and then the other.

Happy with his progress, I looked over at his owner and said, "Give him another fifteen or twenty minutes, and I think we'll have him." By that I meant he'd probably be loading all by himself by then.

I had just finished saying that when three men appeared out of nowhere. One was a tall, thin man wearing a straw cowboy hat. The other two were short and stocky men wearing baseball caps. All three were standing about twenty-five feet away, watching intently with their arms folded across their chests.

They had been there less than two minutes when the tall one said flatly, "Trying to load him that way is going to take all day."

"It doesn't matter to me," I said, half joking and half serious. "I've got nothing else to do till dark." All three seemed to shake their heads in disgust as they turned to walk away, only to return a few minutes later.

"Here," the tall one said loudly. "We'll load that jughead for you."

"No, thanks," I replied in protest. But before I could even get the words out, all three were directly behind the horse. The tall one took his hat off and slapped the horse's backside with it. "Get in there you son of a bitch," he yelled.

"Hey," I shouted. "Knock it off!"

"Pull on his head," one of the short men said, as all three of them slammed into the horse from behind with their shoulders. The horse, which was now in a full-blown panic, was knocked off his front feet, landing on his knees inside the trailer.

"Pull on his head," the man repeated. "He'll go in."

As he said that, the horse began to thrash around trying to back out. I grabbed his halter and pulled directly upwards to help him to his feet.

"Get away from him," I yelled. "Let him out!" The tall man climbed in the trailer and took the rope right out of my hands.

"Come on," he said, looking at me. "Help pull. You want this horse in the trailer or not!"

To say that I was mad would be an understatement. I was furious. Their assistance had been unsolicited and unwanted, and still they had taken it upon themselves to force their way into the situation.

Now, not only had they ruined the trust that the horse had built up in me, but also any chances of the horse wanting to load any time soon. They had just made my job five times harder than it needed to be, and all because they figured that the method that I was using was taking too long. Even though they had no stake in what was going on, their impatience had gotten the better of them, and they just couldn't help but jump in to try to speed the process up.

"No," I said sarcastically. "I think three people beating on this one horse is more than enough. You don't need me for this." With that I walked out of the trailer and up to the horse's owner.

"If you want to try this again when Curly, Moe, and Larry aren't around, I'll be happy to help," I told her flatly. "Otherwise, I don't believe I want to waste any more of my time or the horse's."

I climbed into my pickup and drove away. It was the only sensible thing to do. I was certain that if I stood and watched the remainder of what those three thugs were doing to that horse, there was no question that I'd lose my temper, and that wouldn't have done anybody any good.

I have to admit, though, what happened that day was a perfect example of how people get in trouble when trying to load horses in trailers. They look at what they're doing from their point of view and not the horse's. Instead of taking the time they need to do the job right, they begin to lose their patience after a short period and try to force matters. Then what happens is that a job that should have taken an hour or less ends up not getting done at all, or the problem ends up being worse than when they started.

———————

I learned a long time ago that when it comes to trailer loading, you have to have the proper mindset before you start. You also have to give yourself enough time to do the job right. For me, having the proper mindset means trying to understand what has caused the horse to become hard to load to begin with and then trying to overcome the problem without using force.

For instance, I remember a horse some time ago that was a little bit on the spoiled side. He would walk up to the trailer without any trouble. He'd even put his front feet in. The one thing he wouldn't do was put his back feet in. He would stand that way—front end in, back end out—all day without trying to load.

His owner had tried everything she knew to try to get that horse's back end in the trailer. She had hit him with whips and leather straps. She had poked him with sharp sticks. She had even used a butt rope and tried to force him in. Nothing had worked.

When I arrived, I found the same thing. The horse would load his front end without hesitation but absolutely refused to put his back end in. Somehow, we needed to motivate him to move his back end, which up until then had proven to be impossible. I went to my truck and brought back a small training tool that I'd used in similar situations. The tool was nothing more than a brown paper grocery sack, inside a plastic grocery sack attached to the end of a five-foot fiberglass whip handle.

Normally, all it takes to get a horse's attention is to shake the thing lightly on the ground behind him. As I did this, the horse sleepily turned his head in my direction but otherwise didn't appear to be concerned. I shook it a little more vigorously. Still no reaction. I moved a little closer and tried again. This time he turned to look at me with a little different expression, an expression that told me that he was finally becoming concerned with the unfamiliar sight and sound of the object.

I continued shaking the thing while slowly approaching him. It wasn't until I was within about fifteen feet of his back end that he finally offered to move a back leg. When he did, however, it was a big offer. He picked the left foot up and put it right in the trailer. I immediately stopped shaking the sacks and took a few steps backwards to show him that what he had just done was exactly what I was looking for.

I allowed him to stand for a few minutes, then began to approach him once again. This time I had no sooner started shaking the sacks than he quickly picked up the other foot and hopped into the trailer. As before, I immediately stopped what I was doing and backed up. His owner, who was standing next to him inside the trailer, quickly began praising and petting him to give him an even bigger reward for doing the right thing.

We let him stand inside for a few minutes, backed him out, and started all over. Each time we loaded him after that, we gave him the opportunity to put his back end in on his own. If he stalled, I would immediately begin to shake the sacks, and each time he would respond by jumping in. In less than an hour's time, he had become so conditioned that loading all four feet was simply second nature. He had learned that if the front feet go in, so do the back. If the back feet didn't go in, we started to make that annoying sound behind him. He decided that it was easier to load than to have to put up with that noise.

As a rule, I have found that the little tool works quite well on horses with the same or very similar loading problems. Even then, though, it doesn't work on all of them.

I had one horse with the exact same problem that I treated in the exact same way and got no response whatsoever. With that horse, I could even go up and tap him with the sacks on the butt, legs, and flank, and he still remained completely oblivious. Finally, I decided to try something that I'd seen the old man do years ago. The difference was that he was teaching a stubborn horse that didn't want to lead how to go forward. The technique had worked quite well in that situation, and frankly, I couldn't see why it wouldn't work here.

I backed the horse's front end out of the trailer and loosely tied a lead rope around his neck. I then tied several pieces of baling twine together end-to-end until I had one piece about fifteen feet long. In one end I tied a loop about six inches in diameter, and in the other end I tied a large knot. I tied another piece of twine about six feet long to the looped end and then placed the horse's tail in the loop. I slid the loop clear up to the base of the horse's tail, where the tail meets the body, and slipped the knotted end under the lead rope that was tied around the horse's neck.

I then asked the horse to load. As expected, he put his front end in, but refused to go any farther. By this time I was holding onto the knotted end of the baling twine with my left hand and the short piece of twine that was tied to the loop under the horse's tail with my right. I began to kiss to the horse, a signal that I wanted him to go forward. He simply

He quickly picked up the other foot and hopped into the trailer.

ignored me. I then began to slowly pull on the knotted end of the twine. This, in turn, put tension on the loop that was under his tail.

He quickly began to tuck his butt underneath himself in an effort to get away from the sensation that the loop was causing. It was of no use though. I continued to apply pressure until the sensation became too much. He jumped in the trailer trying to get away from it. I immediately dropped the knotted end of the twine to release the pressure. However, he had clamped his tail down tight against the loop, causing the sensation to continue. At that point, I pulled hard on the twine that was in my right hand and attached to the loop, dislodging it from under his tail.

I let him stand quietly in the trailer for some time before backing him out and starting all over. In fifteen minutes time, by working in the same way, he was loading by himself. I merely had to lead him up to the open trailer, kiss to him, and in he'd go.

The good thing about a spoiled horse that only goes halfway in a trailer is that half of the work is already done. At least he's loading his front end. After that, it's simply a matter of finding a way to get the back end in, without traumatizing him in the process. With other spoiled horses, the task is a little more difficult.

The worst horse I ever had to deal with, as far as trailer loading, was a big Tennessee walker named Duke. Duke's behavior was the epitome of everything that could possibly go wrong when trying to get a horse into a two-horse trailer. I couldn't get him any closer to the thing than about fifteen feet before he would begin to protest. He'd do this by stopping dead in his tracks and refusing to go any farther. If I pressed the matter, insisting that he continue on, he'd simply rear up or try to pull back. It was obvious that I needed to take this option away from him and do it as quickly as possible.

As he was rearing for the fourth time, I decided to make my move. While he was still in the air, I struck a dominant and menacing posture. I stood up straight, arms raised over my head, hissing through my teeth, and vigorously shaking the lead rope. This aggressive attitude on my part took him completely by surprise. He immediately got his front feet on the ground and began backing up in an attempt to get as far away from me as he could.

As he backed, I continued my aggressive actions. While doing this, I also carefully watched him, looking for the slightest signal that he'd had enough and was looking for a way to get me to stop. As a rule, this signal comes in the form of a slowing of the horse's backward movement or a cautious glance in your direction. In this case, it was a glance. The second I noticed his offer, I stopped everything that I was doing and let him stand and rest. I gave him a few seconds to relax and think about it before heading back towards the trailer.

Once again, we had gotten within about fifteen feet of the trailer when he stopped and reared. In response, I once again struck my aggressive posture and began backing him up. This needed to be repeated several more times within the next thirty minutes before he finally got the message. The message was that any time he reared or pulled back, I got pretty unfriendly. If he moved forward like I asked, things remained calm and nonthreatening.

I quickly found, however, that just because I was able to get him to approach the trailer, it didn't necessarily mean my problems were over. He simply reached into his bag of tricks and pulled out another of his many well-thought-out and practiced detours, the ones that had kept him out of trailers for the past five years.

As we got within about three feet of the open trailer door, he nonchalantly veered off, dragging me with him. I pulled his head around as best I could, circled him, then brought him back to the trailer. Again, he veered off.

We repeated this several times before I finally decided that I'd had enough. I went to the truck and got my little training tool. You know, the sacks attached to the whip handle. I then came back and tried again.

As we approached the trailer, I could see him preparing to veer off to the right, just as he had every other time we approached. This time, however, I slid the whip handle under his chin so that the sacks suddenly appeared in front of his right eye. Startled, he shied one step to the left, then stopped to get a look at the thing. He looked at it for only a short time before deciding that it didn't pose a threat. He turned to his right and began to walk right at it. I, in turn, began to tap him lightly in the face with the sacks.

In an attempt to get away from the irritating feel and sound that the sacks made as they touched him, he turned to his left and tried to walk past me. I immediately brought the sacks around to his left side and began tapping him with them. This, as expected, turned his head back to the right, where again I met him with the sacks. By working him in this way and leading him forward at the same time, we were soon standing at the door of the trailer.

I let him stand quietly for a few minutes before slowly backing him away and starting all over. It would be another thirty minutes before he would approach the trailer without trying to veer off and without me having to use the sacks to steer him. At this point we had been working for a little over an hour and had just now reached the trailer door.

In most cases, I would look at a horse that I'd been working with for that long and probably quit for the day, giving him time to relax and think about what we'd done. However, I got the distinct impression from this particular horse that he would look at us stopping as a victory on his part. I say this because in the past he had always been able to get the person who was working with him to stop before he got in the trailer. If I stopped now,

I would be no different from everybody else who had worked with him and I would have done nothing to fix this problem.

With that thought in mind, I decided to continue on. I let him stand quietly at the door before asking him to step forward into the right compartment of the trailer. I did this by lightly applying pressure on the lead rope while standing in the left compartment. He defiantly leaned backwards for a few short seconds, then violently reared straight up in the air.

I jumped out of the trailer like I'd been shot out of a gun, shaking the lead rope, hissing, and swinging my arms above my head. As before, this forced him backwards. When he stopped, we tried again.

Again, he reared as I asked him to load, and again he received the same response from me. This went on for nearly twenty minutes before he finally decided to try to move forward instead of back. When he did, it was little more than a shift of his weight, but still enough to warrant a reward from me in the form of a release of the pressure and lavish petting on his shoulder and neck.

We continued to work in this same way for quite a while with my asking for some movement and his giving it to me a little bit at a time. Periodically I would take him away from the trailer and allow him to rest and clear his head. This was also meant as a reward for doing the right thing, offering forward movement.

Finally, after working for nearly two hours, he began to lift a front leg in an attempt to place it on the trailer floor. It was still another fifteen minutes before he actually placed the foot in the trailer. However, even then, it was only to paw at the floor's rubber mat four or five times before taking the foot back out. I looked at this as a tremendous try on his part and rewarded him by taking him away from the trailer for about two minutes. It was another ten minutes after that before he placed the foot on the floor and put some weight on it, and still another twenty minutes before he would put the other front foot in at the same time.

After nearly three hours, we had finally gotten his front end in the trailer. At that point, I took him away from the trailer and let him stand tied for about fifteen minutes. This gave both him and me a break from what we were doing. When we returned, he approached the trailer and even loaded his front end with very little hesitation. I backed him out and reloaded his front end several more times before finally asking him to load his back end.

I did this by kissing to him while at the same time putting forward pressure on the lead rope. After fifteen minutes he hadn't even attempted to move his back end. I once again pulled out my little training tool and began to shake it lightly behind him. He took one look at the sacks and loaded his back end almost immediately.

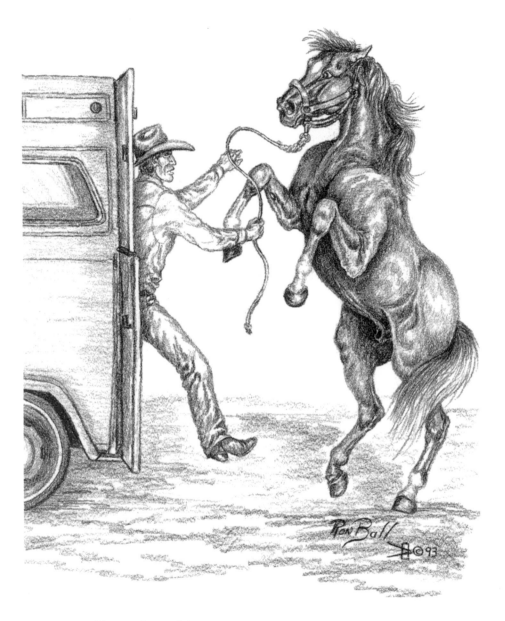

I jumped out of the trailer like I'd been shot out of a gun.

It had taken three-and-a-half hours, start to finish, to go from having a horse that wouldn't get within fifteen feet of the trailer, to having him actually load without a fight. Finally it was time to quit for the day. As I was leading the horse back to his corral, I was approached by a couple of people who had been watching, off and on, throughout the morning.

"You sure have a lot of patience," one of them said. "I would have given up on that horse a long time ago."

"Yeah," the other chimed in. "How can you stand to work with a horse like that for so long without losing your temper?"

"Well," I started to explain, "he didn't give me any reason to lose my temper, because he didn't do anything that I didn't expect him to do. I knew before I even got here today that this horse wasn't going to want to load. So why should I have expected him to within the first few minutes, or hours for that matter?"

I went on to explain that in situations like this, I literally come in thinking that it's going to take all day to get the job done. That way if it only takes a couple of hours, I'm ahead of the game. But I don't get discouraged if it does take all day, because that's what I'd planned on to begin with.

"It's when I put high expectations on myself and the horse that I begin to run into trouble," I told them. "If I keep my expectations low, things usually work out for the best in a relatively short period of time."

The way I looked at this particular horse was that three-and-a-half hours to get him loaded in a trailer was no time at all in comparison to the five years that he'd been able to avoid loading altogether.

"It's all in the way that you look at it," I said, turning the horse loose in his corral.

I've always found it extremely interesting that horse owners will spend days, weeks, and even months teaching their horses desirable behavior. That is, behavior such as how to longe properly, how to pick up the correct leads, or how to turn, stop, and back. But when it comes to getting in a trailer, they expect the horse to learn it in fifteen minutes or less. When he doesn't, the horse is immediately subjected to whatever force the owner deems necessary, whether it be whips, boards, or butt ropes.

I learned my lesson years ago about the dangers of using force. While trying to get a horse into a trailer by using a butt rope, the horse panicked and tried to back out of the trailer. The butt rope was secured to one side of the trailer. I was holding the other end of the rope, which was wrapped around the door jam on the other side of the trailer. The horse became even more panicked when he found he was trapped inside. Because the butt rope was secured tightly behind him, it allowed him very little backward movement. He reared up inside the trailer, tearing the hide off his forehead.

As I worked to try to release my end of the rope, he continued to rear and thrash around, banging himself up even more. When he finally felt the rope behind him loosen, he shot backwards, rearing high in the air as he exited the trailer. He came down, impaling his chest on the trailer's door latch, which like most two-horse trailers was welded to the center partition of the trailer.

It was a terrible wreck and one that I will never forget as long as I live. It was also the very last time I used a butt rope or any other similar kind of force to get a horse to load into a trailer. Since that time, I have worked with countless numbers of horses on trailer loading. Included in these were ten or twelve horses that had been in wrecks while being hauled, several that were severely spoiled, and one that had been in a trailer when it was hit by lightning.

In none of the hundreds of cases that I've dealt with was force used to get the horse to load. Instead, I have spent my time trying to figure out ways to calm down frightened horses, motivate disinterested horses, and take away undesirable options from evasive horses. In other words, I have tried to find ways to communicate what I want from the horse without traumatizing him in the meantime. I have also made it a point to work with each horse as an individual, using different loading techniques for different loading problems.

I recall doing a clinic in which four problem horses were brought in. The first was a sorrel quarter horse gelding that would get within about two feet of the trailer door, then rear and back away. The horse showed no sign of being afraid, but rather appeared to be doing it because that was what he'd been able to get away with in the past. I led him up to the trailer four different times, and each time he reacted the same way.

On the fifth try, as soon as he reared, I struck my menacing posture and began backing him. Shocked, he backed for several feet before showing me he'd had enough by trying to slow down. I then stopped what I was doing, let him stand quietly for a few seconds, and tried again.

For the next three tries, he did the same thing, rearing and backing. I, in turn, would follow him with my menacing posture. On the fourth approach, he stopped and stood quietly at the door. I let him rest there for a few minutes while petting him on the neck before leading him away from the trailer. We approached several more times without him trying to rear. About the fifteenth or sixteenth time that we approached, I kissed to him at the door, asking him to continue forward. He hesitated for a second and then walked right in.

We continued to load and unload the horse for the next thirty minutes, each time taking him away from the trailer before asking him to load again. Each time he simply became more comfortable with what we were doing until finally it became second nature. Start to finish, it had taken us forty minutes to fix this horse's loading problem.

We weren't so lucky with the next one, a black Morgan/Arab cross. She also reared and backed away from the trailer as we approached, but she did it for a different reason. She was scared. As we got closer to the trailer door, she would begin to show the signs—tight lips, alert ears, and quick, jerky movements. By the time we reached the door, her fear became too much, and she'd suddenly rear and back up.

Unlike the first horse, I simply allowed her to back until she decided to stop. I then let her stand for a few seconds before approaching the trailer again. For the next twenty minutes this is all we did—back away from the trailer, stand, then go right back. While doing this, I was asked by a spectator why I didn't respond to this horse's backing like I did with the first horse. The answer was simple. We were dealing with different causes of the problem.

The first horse showed none of the signs of being afraid of the trailer or of approaching the trailer. He had chosen rearing and backing as a way to avoid getting in, simply because that's what he had gotten away with in the past. In a sense, he'd been inadvertently taught that when he got near the open door of a trailer he was supposed to rear. In his case, we had to teach him that rearing and backing away weren't what we wanted. We took that option away from him by making it uncomfortable for him to do it.

The second horse, however, was a different story. She was already uncomfortable. Making her more uncomfortable would have only made things worse. The key to getting through to a horse like that is being quiet, consistent, and making every effort to be non-threatening. By doing just that, I'd been able to communicate to her that I wasn't trying to harm her, and after about twenty minutes, she was finally standing quietly at the open trailer door.

The reason that she was uncomfortable became apparent while she was standing at the door. One of the spectators needed to cross behind her as he made his way to the nearby restroom. Even though he was no closer than thirty feet when he passed, the horse immediately became upset. I took this as a signal from her that she expected the man to come up and beat on her, trying to force her to get into the trailer.

So, for the rest of that session, we made an extra effort to see that no one else passed behind her. We did this to reinforce the fact that we weren't there to harm her, but rather were trying to work with her. The rest of the session, while time consuming, went quite well. By working slowly and rewarding the slightest offer to do what I was asking, she was loading by herself in about an hour and fifteen minutes.

132

In complete contrast, the third horse, a six-year-old mustang mare that had been broke as a two-year-old, walked right up to the trailer and stuck her head inside the left compartment but refused to go any farther. She was completely indifferent to the trailer and any attempts I made to ask her to load.

For this horse, I brought out my little training tool and stood about ten feet directly behind her while her owner climbed in the right-side compartment. He began to ask her to load by applying forward pressure on the lead rope while I started to shake the sacks on the ground from behind. This got her attention immediately, and she responded by swinging her butt from side to side. I moved with her, staying directly behind her and shaking the sacks. If she offered any forward movement, I stopped the shaking and at the same time her owner released the pressure on her lead rope. Less than five minutes after we started, by being consistent each time we asked the horse, she had willingly loaded by herself.

The fourth horse had a problem completely different from the first three. That horse, a small Arab mare, loaded willingly and without hesitation. Her problem came when I asked her to back out. She simply wouldn't do it. The only way we could get her out of the trailer once she was in was to remove the center partition, turn her around, and take her out head first.

Her problem stemmed from the fact that while she had been taught to load, nobody had spent the time to teach her how to unload. With her, the solution was easy. All we needed to do was slow her down some by loading her a little bit at a time, instead of all at once. What I did was ask her to put one front foot in, then take it back out. We did this several times before I asked her to put her other front foot in as well. Again, I backed her out.

Then I asked her to load half way, stop, and back out several times before finally loading her hind feet. When I asked her to back out, she hesitated for a few seconds, then tentatively put first one back foot on the ground, then the other. Standing with both back feet outside the trailer, she hesitated once more before coming out the rest of the way.

Just like that her problem was over.

Looking at these four horses and their individual problems, it's easy to see why different methods needed to be used to accomplish basically the same thing. Each horse is an individual and sees things in his own way. For us to get through to the horse successfully, we have to try to see things from his point of view and then work with him that way.

One of the things I have come to understand about getting a horse into a two-horse trailer is that it only becomes a big deal when we make it a big deal. You can get a lot more done by being calm, reassuring, and confident, than you ever will by losing your temper and hollering like a banshee. The thing to remember here is easy: if you lose your temper, you'll lose the horse. Simple as that.

There are many people out there, however, who swear up and down that the only way to get a horse into a two-horse trailer is to use force. Well, as far as I'm concerned, those people may as well stick their head in a bucket and whack it with a hammer. Using force makes about the same amount of sense. Not only that, but chances are if you use force once, you'll have to use it every time after that. Instead of having a horse that walks in willingly, you've got a ten-round wrestling match that takes over an hour any time you need to go anywhere.

There is no question that trying to teach a horse to load, especially a horse that has had problems in the past, is time consuming. But, if you take your time, are patient, and think through the problem instead of forcing the issue, it's only time consuming once.

NOTES FOR TRAILER LOADING

I think one of the single most common stumbling blocks for a lot of horse people is learning how to quietly, effectively, and comfortably get their horse to load into a trailer. I remember when first writing this chapter I felt I wanted to give some varied examples of how to load a horse, while at the same time giving an example or two of what not to do.

I've received many letters from folks over the years specifically about this chapter. It was great to hear how, after reading it, so many people have come to the understanding that there are almost as many ways to load a horse that is having trouble as there are horses that are having trouble. I've had a lot of people tell me how, after reading this chapter, they were able to slow down a little and eventually find innovative ways to quietly get their horses to load. It truly makes me feel good to know that reading something I wrote was the catalyst for them to search for, and ultimately find, a way to help both them and their horse.

Mounting problems

As I was leaning against the arena fence, I talked with my new client, Kelly. She had raised and trained the horse we were to work with herself. Because it had been the first time she had attempted something like that, she'd run into a few problems she needed help with.

I stayed outside the arena as she took the horse in and got ready to mount. No sooner had she gotten inside than I was approached by a nervous-acting little fellow who had been saddling his horse nearby.

"Are you Mark Rashid, the trainer?" he asked quickly.

"Yes, I am," I replied, offering my hand.

"Hi," he chirped. "I'm Keith. I'm in the horse game myself, you know."

"Horse game?" I questioned.

"Yeah," he replied. "You know, riding, training. You know, that sort of thing."

"I see," I said. "The horse game."

"Yeah, you know, the horse game," he fired back. "Like you."

"Like me," I said cautiously.

"Yeah," he said, putting one foot up on the bottom rail of the fence, tipping his brand new Stetson hat back on his head and leaning next to me. "You know, I been watching this little gal, and just between you, me, and the fence post, she needs help. You know what I mean? A lot of help."

"I know," I replied. "That's why I'm ..."

"I told her I'd be happy to give her a hand," he interrupted, "but I guess she'd already talked to you, you know."

"I see," I said, turning back towards the arena.

"Watch this," he said, talking so quickly that it was a little difficult to understand him. "This horse doesn't even stand still long enough for her to get on, you know what I mean. Watch."

I couldn't help but look at the nervous little fellow for a second, wondering if he was on some kind of drug or if he just talked that way naturally.

"It takes her forever to get on this horse, you know," he repeated. "The horse doesn't stand still. It takes forever. Watch."

I had to smile as I turned my attention back to the arena. As I did, Kelly was trying to get on the horse. It was true. Each time she tried to put her foot in the stirrup, the horse did try to walk off. It took a good half dozen tries before she was finally able to get herself up in the saddle.

"See what I mean? See what I mean?" Keith blurted. "I told you. Boy, I'd never own a horse like that, you know. Would you? I never would, you know."

"Well, actually," I said, half chuckling, "I don't think this is that big of a deal. In fact, I think we can probably fix that pretty quickly."

"Yeah, well, maybe," he replied. "I'll tell you one thing though. I'd never own a horse like that, you know. A horse that walks off like that."

I nodded my head, not knowing how else to answer him.

"Well," he said, grabbing my hand and shaking it. "I guess you've got your work cut out for you, you know. I'll let you get to work. Nice talking to you. Sometime, maybe we can sit down and compare notes, you know."

"On the horse game?" I questioned.

"Yeah," he replied, with a big smile. "The horse game, you know. Well, nice talking to you."

"Nice talking with you," I said, smiling to myself. I went into the arena and walked up to where Kelly was sitting quietly on her horse.

"What did he want?" she asked, nodding her head in Keith's direction. "To tell you how bad a horse I have?"

"No," I smiled. "We were just talking about the horse game." Apparently Kelly hadn't taken her conversations with Keith as lightheartedly as I had.

"He bugs me," she said.

"Oh," I said, still smiling, "I think he means well. Besides, he appears to be pretty harmless."

"I suppose," Kelly said, after thinking about it for a while. "But he still bugs me."

"Let's forget about him and start thinking about this horse," I told her. "First things first. Let's fix your mounting problem."

With that, I had her get down and pull her saddle and saddle pad off the horse. I explained to her that I've found horses to be hard to mount for one of two reasons. Either a horse has soreness somewhere and doesn't want you to get on his back because it hurts to have you up there, or he just hasn't been taught how to stand still when you get on to begin with.

"Obviously," I told her, "if the horse is sore or if the tack doesn't fit right, we need to find that out first."

With the saddle off, I slowly pressed along the horse's spine with my finger tips and the heel of my hand. I then checked his withers, neck, shoulders, and hips for soreness but found none anywhere. Then, without the saddle pad, I placed the saddle on the horse's back to make sure it fit his back properly. I could see no place where it appeared to be binding him up or hurting him in any way, so we saddled him back up.

"Okay," I said. "Why don't you try to get on, and we'll see if we can find the problem." She stuck her foot in the stirrup, accidentally kicking the horse with the toe of her boot. Immediately, the horse began to walk off.

"Well," I said, explaining what she had just done. "I think that's part of the problem. However, even if you hadn't kicked him, he would have had to move anyway because his legs weren't squared up underneath him either. As soon as you put weight in the stirrup, you'll pull him off balance, forcing him to move just so he doesn't fall over."

This time, before trying to get on, I had her pull the stirrup towards her three or four times until the horse began to brace himself naturally against the pressure.

"There," I told her. "Now he won't fall over when you put your weight in the stirrup."

With the horse's feet squared up underneath himself and being careful not to kick him when she put her foot in the stirrup, she again tried to mount. Almost immediately, the horse began to walk off. Kelly took her foot out of the stirrup, turned, and looked at me with an expression of disgust on her face.

Almost immediately, the horse began to walk off.

"That sure worked good," she said sarcastically.

"Okay," I smiled. "Take it easy. You have to understand something here. The entire time that you've been working with this horse, he's been allowed to walk off whenever you've tried to get on. Because of that, he thinks that's what he's supposed to do. We now have to show him that isn't right."

"How are we going to do that?" she questioned.

"As soon as he starts to walk off, take the slack out of your left rein and bring his head around," I told her. "This will cause him to circle around you. Let him circle until he decides to stop. Then give him his head back. Pet him to let him know that standing still is what you want. Then start all over."

For the next ten minutes, she did exactly that. By the end of that time, she had successfully taught the horse to stand still when she put weight in the stirrup. However, I noticed as she began to throw a leg over that she not only dragged her foot across the horse's rump, but also unceremoniously dropped all of her weight in the saddle as well—both things that will cause a horse to walk off before a rider is ready.

For another five minutes, Kelly practiced getting in the saddle more smoothly. Each time, if the horse tried to walk off, she brought his head around, causing him to circle. In no time at all, she could get on and off the horse without him even offering to move. We then took him out of the arena and led him around for about fifteen minutes. This gave him a break from what we were doing and also let us see if he had retained what we'd just taught him.

While we were walking, I explained to Kelly that when a horse moves off when a rider is trying to mount, most people just pull straight back on the reins to get him to stop, like she had. This usually will get the horse to stop, all right, but doesn't teach the horse to stand still.

"What you're doing, by circling the horse around you," I pointed out, "is making walking away more difficult than standing still. You're just giving him the opportunity to decide for himself what's easier."

After returning to the arena, Kelly first pulled on the stirrup to set her horse's feet. She then put her foot in the stirrup and bounced up and down three or four times. The horse didn't even flinch. As she lifted herself up into the saddle, he shifted his weight to compensate for her but otherwise didn't move.

She got off and on five more times, each time with the same result. I then told her that would be enough for one day and we could go ahead and put him away.

As we were making our way to the gate, Keith, the little fellow I had met earlier, brought his horse in. It was a very nice-looking, bay quarter horse mare wearing an equally impressive-looking saddle. The saddle, however, appeared not to fit her very well and was riding right down on her withers.

He took the horse out to the middle of the arena, tightened the cinch, and tried to get on. The horse immediately moved forward and to the right, away from him. As his foot popped out of the stirrup, he jerked back hard on the reins to get the horse to stop. It took him five tries finally to get in the saddle, and even then the horse appeared uncomfortable, tossing her head, pawing at the ground, and prancing in place.

By that time we had already made our way out of the arena and had tied Kelly's horse to a nearby hitch rail. Kelly had just started pulling her tack off when Keith rode up to the arena fence.

"Hey, Mark," he said, as his horse tossed her head and blew hard through her nose. "Hey, how do you like this horse? Nice, huh? She's pretty nice, don't you think?"

"Yes," I replied, "she's a real nice-looking horse."

"Yup," he grinned. "She's five years old, you know, and I'm the only one that's ever rode her. The only one. Pretty nice, huh?"

As I walked over to the arena fence to get a better look at her, I noticed that under her saddle was a cut-back pad, a pad that allows the withers of high-withered horses to be exposed. It's a pad that is designed to relieve the pressure a low-fitting saddle may cause to a horse like that.

Unfortunately, he had the saddle cinched so tight and it fit her so poorly that its gullet was riding directly on her withers, which appeared to be causing her excruciating pain.

"She's a great horse," he beamed. "A great horse, you know. Just the kind I like, you know what I mean?"

"I know what you mean," I replied. "I was wondering though. I noticed that when you were trying to get on, that she kind of moved away a couple of times. Does she do that all the time?"

"Moved away?" he questioned. "Oh, moved away. I know what you mean. You mean when I was trying to get on. I see. Well, that's because she's got a lot of spirit. A lot of spirit, you know. That's how I train 'em. I train 'em to have a lot of get-up-and-go, you know. I don't like a deadhead horse."

"I see," I said, nodding my head. "I thought maybe she might be sore backed or something. I mean, I thought you said you didn't like horses that walked off when you tried to get on, and I know that sometimes soreness will cause . . ."

"No, no," he interrupted. "It's nothing like that. No soreness here, you know. That's just the way I train 'em. I train 'em to have a lot of get-up-and-go, you know. You know what I mean. A lot of spirit. That's how I train 'em."

"I see," I said. "Well, nice talking to you again."

"Nice talking to you, too," he replied. "Don't worry, no soreness here. A lot of spirit, that's all. A lot of spirit, get-up-and-go. That's all, you know."

"Sure," I said, trying not to sound patronizing. "See you later."

"Yup, see you later," he replied, turning his horse and riding off.

The next week, Kelly moved her horse to a different boarding stable, and we continued working with him there, so I had no reason to believe that I'd ever see or talk with Keith again. Much to my surprise, however, I received a phone call from him about seven months later. It seemed that his horse had developed a couple of problems he was having trouble getting through, and he wondered if I might be willing to come and have a look at her. I told him I'd be happy to.

Upon having a look at the mare, I quickly found that she had more than just a couple of problems. To tell the truth, she had developed just about every problem you could imagine, from being hard to catch, not accepting the bit, and biting when you tried to cinch her, to not letting you mount and bucking with you once you were on.

Having a pretty good idea of what had caused the problems, I first checked her back for soreness. I found her to be in pain from her withers back to her hips, with the greatest amount of pain in the area of the withers. She was also quite sore on the left side of her neck, as well as having some small but visible sores in the corners of her mouth, obviously caused by the bit.

Keith's speech and movements were visibly more subdued as I showed him how sore her back had become.

"What can I do to fix this?" he asked quietly.

"Well," I told him, "before we can do anything, we first need to get her feeling better."

I suggested talking to either his vet or a chiropractor to find out what would be the best way to get rid of the soreness. When the soreness was gone, we'd have another look at her and go from there. I also told him that I thought his saddle may have been the source of these problems to begin with and that he might want to consider finding one that fit her a little better. Surprisingly enough, he was very receptive to all the suggestions and told me that he would do whatever it took to get her back on the right track.

Two more months passed before I heard from Keith again. He told me that he had been working very closely with a chiropractor who had all but eliminated his horse's soreness problems. With the chiropractor's okay, he had been riding the horse for the past two weeks. He had also gotten a new saddle that fit her a lot better, and as a result, most of her problems had disappeared.

The two things he was still having trouble with were her biting when he tried to cinch her up and her moving away when he tried to get on. (I have to admit, I found it interesting that only nine months earlier he saw her walking off when he tried to mount as her having "spirit" and "get-up-and-go." Now he saw it as a problem. I guess that's the way it is, though. A problem isn't really a problem until you perceive it as such.) Regardless, he now wanted a hand trying to remedy the remaining problems, and I was more than happy to try to help.

When I arrived at the stable, the horse was already caught and tied to a hitch rail near the arena, and Keith was quietly grooming her. When he finished, I put the saddle pad and saddle gently on her back. Immediately, her head came up, and her eye changed from being half closed to wide open.

I'd already explained to Keith that the reason she'd been biting when he cinched her was probably due, first, to cinching her too tight and, second, because in the past it had caused her back to hurt. She probably started biting out of self-defense, but as time went on, it had turned into a habit.

As she began to raise her head, I pointed it out to Keith.

"See this," I said. "She's already getting concerned and all I've done was set the saddle on her back."

"Yup," he blurted, "I sure do. You bet. Sure do. I see it."

"We're going to have to do two things here," I told him. "First, we have to take away her reason for biting. What I'll do is cinch her just tight enough to keep the saddle from slipping off her back, and no more. That way we can start to show her that she's no longer going to be hurt every time we draw the cinch up."

"Yup, that makes sense," he said. "Sure does. Makes a lot of sense. I see. No tight cinch. Got it."

"The second thing we're going to do," I continued, "is take away her biting option. I'm going to do that by sticking my elbow towards her head as she brings it around to bite me. What will happen is, instead of getting a bite out of me, she'll run into something hard—my elbow. This way we can stop her from biting before she starts."

"Right," he blurted again. "Elbow out. Stop her before she starts. Makes sense. Elbow out. Good idea. Got it."

Smiling to myself, I slowly reached under her belly and got ahold of the cinch, which was hanging down on the other side. I brought the cinch up and slid the latigo through the cinch ring, back up through the saddle ring, and began to pull it tight. I had no sooner begun to apply the light pressure than, as expected, she turned and tried to bite. Luckily, I caught the movement of her head out of the corner of my eye and met it with my bent elbow. She hit my elbow soundly with the end of her nose and immediately withdrew.

I let her stand quietly and stroked her neck for a few minutes before loosening the cinch and starting all over. Having tried to bite me about a half dozen times over the next five minutes and running into my bent elbow each time, she finally decided to quit.

The next thirty minutes were spent doing nothing more than gently tightening then loosening the cinch. In fact, for the next three days, all we did with her was put the saddle on, tighten the cinch, and take the saddle off. Only when I was certain that she was completely comfortable with being cinched up and that there was no longer a likelihood of her trying to bite, did we start on her mounting problem.

"What I'm going to do here," I explained to Keith, as we led the mare into the arena, "is to try to show her that what we want is for her to stand still. In other words, we're going to make it harder on her to move away than it is to stand."

"You bet," he said. "I understand. No problem. Make it harder to move than to stand still. Got it."

With that I reached up and tried to put my foot in the stirrup. The horse jumped to her right, away from me, and moved about four steps before stopping. I brought her back to where we started and tried again. She did the same thing again. On the third try when she jumped away, I raised my arms above my head and hissed through my teeth, which was enough to startle her. It also caused her to backpedal about twenty feet before stopping. I let her stand quietly for a few seconds and petted her on her neck before taking her back to the center and trying again. She blew sideways two more times as I tried to put my foot in the stirrup, and both times she received the same response from me.

On the fourth try, she appeared nervous as I put my foot in the stirrup, but didn't attempt to move. I kept my foot in the stirrup for only a couple of seconds before taking it back out, putting it on the ground, and giving her a lavish reward of pets and strokes on her head and neck.

After that, I kept my foot in the stirrup just a little longer each time I put it in, until I could have it there for twenty to thirty seconds without her trying to move. Only then did I try to put some weight in the stirrup. As I did that for the first time, she slowly began to walk forward. I, in turn, brought her head around, forcing her to circle around me. She circled only once, with my foot still in the stirrup, before stopping.

I caught the movement of her head out of the corner of my eye.

I kept working with her in this way for the next ten minutes before she would finally set her feet under her when I put weight in the stirrup. By the time I actually sat in the saddle, she stood rock solid, as if she'd never even had a mounting problem to begin with.

"Unbelievable," Keith said, as I pulled myself up in the saddle for the fourth time without her trying to move off. "I would have never thought you could fix that problem that fast, you know. I mean, that was fast. Real fast. Quicker than I thought. You know what I mean?"

"Well," I replied, climbing down out of the saddle. "That's how it goes sometimes. Why don't you give it a try?"

"Me?" he blurted. "Oh, boy. You bet. You bet I will. I just hope I don't screw her up, you know. I mean, now that she's fixed, I hope I don't do something to screw her up. You know what I mean?"

"I know what you mean," I told him, handing him the reins. "Just take it easy with her. Don't be in a hurry. Don't jerk on the reins or kick her in the side when you put your foot in the stirrup. Try not to bump her with your right leg when you swing it over and don't drop your weight in the saddle. Set it down nicely."

The entire time I was talking, he looked directly at me, continuously nodding his head like it was attached to his neck with a spring. When I was finished talking, he repeated what I said, as if he were reciting the answers to an oral quiz.

"Got it," he said, slowly approaching the horse. "Take it easy. Don't hurry. Don't jerk on the reins. Don't kick her. Don't bump her and don't drop my weight. Right. Got it."

"And relax a little bit," I said, smiling. "If you're nervous, she'll be nervous."

"Right. Relax. Deep breath. Got it."

He gently put his foot in the stirrup, bounced up and down three or four times, then cautiously pulled himself up. He stood motionless in the stirrup for a couple of seconds before ever-so-slowly putting his right leg over and sitting in the saddle. He looked down at me with a smile so big that I wasn't sure it would all fit on his face.

"You know," he said in a whisper, "that's the very first time she hasn't tried to move when I got on. The very first time."

"Is that right?" I asked. "Well, that's great. I'm glad we got through to her. By the way, she isn't sleeping so I don't think you'll need to whisper."

"Duh," he said, lightly slapping himself in the forehead and letting out a genuinely hearty laugh. "Yeah, don't want to wake her up."

For the next half hour, he practiced getting on and off, and not once did she try to move away. He finished off the session by riding a few laps at a walk around the arena. Both

MARK RASHID

he and his horse looked very content and happy, as he reached down to pet her on her neck periodically as they went.

Of all the people whom I've worked with over the years, I think Keith is the one that comes to mind most often. Not because of his quick, almost machine-like speech or even his nervous mannerisms, but because of his genuine affection for his horse.

He had made a very great effort to alter his own horse-handling style so he could, in turn, help his horse overcome the problems that he had caused her to develop. This is something that many people wouldn't even think of doing. As a rule, they just see the animal as a problem horse and leave it at that, never thinking that they may have been the cause of the problems to begin with.

The only unfortunate thing about his situation is that it had taken him so long to realize that he was, indeed, causing her problems. Had he seen her original mounting problem as a red flag indicating something was wrong, instead of passing it off as her having spirit, he probably could have avoided the rest of the problems that followed.

The truth of the matter is, if your horse doesn't let you mount, it's usually a sign that something is wrong or is going to be wrong. By fixing the problem right then, or at least acknowledging that there may, in fact, be a problem, there's no telling what kind of calamity you may be avoiding and what kind of stress, aggravation, and pain you can avoid putting your horse through.

NOTES FOR MOUNTING PROBLEMS

In this chapter I discussed a couple things I used to do to help horses that wouldn't stand to be mounted. I realized while reading that the two things I primarily spoke about are on opposite ends of the spectrum as far as the use of pressure or energy goes. One method I spoke about consisted of allowing the horse to walk several circles around the rider and allow the horse to stop and stand on their own, while the other consisted of putting what seemed like a substantial amount of pressure on the horse until it stood still.

While both of these methods do indeed work (assuming the handler's timing, as well as the amount of pressure they use is in accordance with what the horse needs at the time), I realize now that both methods also consist primarily of ideas of things to do after the horse has already moved. They don't really explain how to help the horse find a way to stand still in the first place.

I have found over the years that noticing a horse's "trigger" for wanting to move (the thing that we do that gets them to think about moving), then either altering the thing we are

148

doing slightly, or redirecting the horse's thought before it turns into an action (movement) is often a much more effective way of handling the situation.

I can also see now that one of the things that may have been helpful to address in this chapter would have been teaching a horse how to be mounted from a fence or mounting block. During most of the time leading up to when I wrote this book I had been spending much of my time on various ranches where mounting blocks simply weren't used. As a result, the thought of discussing mounting blocks didn't really even cross my mind. It was only after I began doing clinics that I realized how many people out there not only used mounting blocks, but how many of those people have horses that don't know how to line up to one. So for anyone who was perhaps wondering why there was no mention of mounting blocks in a chapter titled "Mounting Problems" . . . that's why.

Balking

The old man had recently bought a nice-looking but very overweight paint mare. He had turned the mare over to me for exercising and to see if I could thin her down a little. Of course, I was happy to do it.

Behind the barn at his place was a large fenced-off field. The ground was so poor that nothing but a few hardy weeds grew in it, and we used this area mostly for turnouts and a kind of riding arena.

On the day I started working with the mare, the old man walked with me as I led her out. We crossed the wooden foot bridge that spanned the small irrigation ditch and passed through the gate on the north end of the field. It was there that the old man explained that the mare was gate sour and would probably want to stop if I rode her anywhere near it. So, to avoid that, he suggested I keep her down on the south end of the field. We would work on her gate problem another time.

I led her down to the south end, mounted up, and began to work. It was mid-June and a very hot day. As a result, she had already begun sweating and appeared to be very irritable. Because of the heat, we worked only in a walk and slow jog. We'd been at it for nearly an hour when the old man, who was still standing at the gate, called to me telling me that'd be enough.

"Don't ride her over here," he said, referring to bringing her to the gate. "Take her to the middle and get off her there. Then lead her the rest of the way."

"Okay," I replied, waving to him.

Up until that point, we had been riding in large circles down at the south end. But as I headed her in a straight line north to the center of the field, I began to feel a change in her body movements. I felt a tremendous amount of forward energy building up, and although she was still in a walk, I got the feeling that something was about to happen. Evidently the old man could see what I was feeling, because suddenly he yelled, "That's far enough. Get off her right there."

Before I could, though, the mare just blew. She squealed loudly and went into a quick spin to the right. She stopped the spin facing the direction she started and bucked halfheartedly three or four times. Then she took off running for the gate like she was Man-O-War.

She covered the hundred-yard distance to the gate in a matter of seconds, slamming on the brakes and stopping only ten feet short of hitting it. The quick stop took me completely by surprise, and I shot over her head like water over a broken dam.

I hit the ground in front of her and had no sooner lit than the mare's momentum carried her directly over the top of me. She tried to avoid stepping on me but, unfortunately, wasn't successful. Her right front foot came down on my left hand as she ran the rest of the way to the gate.

I'd never had a broken bone before, but after I heard the sickening snap when I was stepped on, I was pretty sure I had one then. In fact, the pain I was experiencing was so severe that I hadn't even noticed that the old man had made his way over and was kneeling next to me.

"Let me see it," he said, trying to get me to stop rolling around on the ground long enough for him to get a look at the hand.

"Give me your hand," I heard him shout. "Come on. Settle down and let me see it." I understood the tone of voice he was using. It was the let-me-see-it-or-else tone, and it got my attention immediately.

I shot over her head like water over a broken dam.

I took a labored deep breath, sat up, and stuck my hand out for him to look at. The pained expression that crossed his face told me right away that something wasn't right, so for the first time, I too looked at the hand. The top of it was already swollen and black-and-blue, and my ring finger was going off at an angle that it was never meant to.

"The break is right here," he said, matter-of-factly, pointing to a spot on the top of my hand next to the knuckle of my ring finger. "I'm going to have to set it."

"What do you mean?" I asked, trying to catch my breath.

"The bone is out of place," he said. "We need to put it back, or it's going to hurt like hell."

"It already hurts like hell," I protested.

"I know," he said, grabbing my wrist with his left hand and the knuckle of my ring finger with his right. "It'll hurt even more if we don't do this. Now take a deep breath."

But even before I could, he pulled on the knuckle, sliding the two bones back in place. The pain was awful, and I felt sick to my stomach and lightheaded at the same time. It took a while, but after I got to feeling a little better, he had me go over and put my hand in the cold water that was running in the irrigation ditch, to keep the swelling down. While I was doing that, he went over and got on the paint mare.

My only consolation as I lay on my belly in the dirt with my broken hand in the ditch was that I figured the horse that put me there would now be taught some manners by the old man. Frankly, I was hoping that he'd really get after her and teach her a lesson she'd never forget. I should have known better.

He got in the saddle, sitting quietly for a few seconds before turning her head and asking her to move off, away from the gate. The horse turned her head but refused to move. He then did something that surprised me a little. With her head turned to the left nearly clear to his boot, he dallied the rein to the saddle horn, reached in his shirt pocket, and casually pulled out a cigarette. He lit it and sat patiently in the saddle, as if waiting for something to happen.

Several minutes passed before the mare finally began to look for a way to get rid of the pressure. She started by leaning to the right. When that didn't work, she tried pulling to the right. When that didn't work, she finally decided to move to the left, the direction the old man had her head to begin with.

As soon as she began to move, he reached down and released the dally, allowing her to straighten out, but only after she was facing south, away from the gate. Almost immediately, though, she attempted to turn back towards the gate. For the next ten minutes, a tremendous battle of wills was waged between the horse that wanted to face the gate and the old man who wanted her away from it.

Finally, the old man's patience and persistence paid off with the mare quietly facing the direction he had been asking her to. After letting her stand and rest for a few minutes, he asked her to move forward, away from the gate. He applied light pressure to her sides with his heels, but the mare ignored him. He continued to ask for some forward movement several times over the next ten minutes without a response. Finally he replaced the pressure he had been applying with his heels with solid and meaningful kicks. Again there was no response. While continuing the kicks, he slapped her lightly on the shoulders with the ends of his reins. Still, no response. He then slapped her harder with the reins, but again it didn't seem to faze her.

With that, he quit everything he was doing and, while once again sitting quietly in the saddle, pulled out another cigarette. He smoked it about halfway down before nonchalantly mashing it out on the saddle horn, picking up the reins, and starting all over.

This time, he went from applying light pressure with his heels to slapping her with the reins in less than about forty-five seconds. This was considerably quicker than the ten minutes it had taken the previous time. As before, however, it seemed to have no effect on the horse, and after slapping her with the reins about a half dozen times, he added something new. He stopped the kicking and rein slapping completely and replaced it with something that I thought not only looked foolish but didn't appear to have anything to do with getting a horse to move forward.

He began very slowly and methodically to move the horse's head from side to side by drawing the reins first one way, then the other. As time went on, the movement became quicker until it appeared that the horse began to lose her balance, causing her to take a step. Immediately the old man stopped the movement. He let her stand quietly for a few seconds, petting her on her neck before starting all over.

By working with her in this way, he had successfully gotten the horse to move about ten feet in the next few minutes. She had also begun to respond to him more quickly. Apparently in an attempt to avoid having her head pulled from side to side, she began moving as soon as he bumped her with his heels. She wasn't moving very far or very fast, but at least she was moving.

Forty-five minutes later, the old man could ride her from the gate to the middle of the field, stop, and then go back to the gate without her stampeding off. Once back at the gate, he could dismount, smoke a cigarette, get back on, and head towards the middle of the field without her even thinking about balking. This was accomplished, all because he had made it harder on her to stand still than to go forward.

The one thing that sticks in my mind about that day, other than the fact that I spent most of it on my belly with my broken hand in an irrigation ditch, is that the old man did not once lose either his patience or his temper with the horse. He had been very deliberate and methodical in what he had done and, as a result, had successfully changed the mare's mind about wanting to stop or stand near the gate.

———————

Since that day, I have seen and worked with quite a few horses with similar problems. By using basically the same attitude and technique that I'd seen the old man use, I'd always been successful at motivating the horse to move when it was apparent that he'd rather not. That is, until I came upon a nineteen-year-old quarter horse gelding named Red.

Red was a pretty interesting horse. He was easy to catch, easy to saddle and bridle, and even easy to mount. He would move off nicely with a little leg pressure, he neck reined well, and he would stop on a dime. However, he had also, over the years, developed a problem that wouldn't surface until you rode him about fifty feet away from the barn.

For no apparent reason other than he didn't seem to want to go any farther, he'd stop dead in his tracks. He was perfectly content to stand in that one spot. He didn't want to go forward and wasn't overly concerned about going back. He seemed totally oblivious to everything and everyone around him, including his rider. A number of things had been used to try to get the horse to move forward, including kicking him with sharp spurs, hitting him with crops, whips, and boards, and even, at one point, shooting him in the backside with a BB gun. Nothing worked. As a last resort before taking the horse to the killers, his owner brought him to me to see if I could fix his problem.

Unfortunately, I soon began to see that Red was not going to be an easy nut to crack. To say that he was determined not to move would be an understatement. It was almost as if it was simply a way of life for him. The same technique that I'd seen the old man use years ago, the technique that had also been so successful for me on countless horses, didn't do anything for this one. Not only had I gotten to the point in the technique where I was bringing his head from side to side, but with this horse, I even began to throw my weight back and forth in the saddle in the opposite direction from his head. I was doing this in an effort to make it as uncomfortable as possible for him to be standing still.

Even that had no effect on him, and I was beginning to see him as a horse that I might not be able to help. In fact, for the first time since I'd begun training horses on my own, I was ready to admit that I wasn't going to be able to get through to this one. That is, until something that the old man said to me years ago came rushing back.

"One of these days," he had told me, "you're going to get a horse that is going to flat make you think nothing that you know to do is going to work on him, so you're going to have to make it up as you go along. What you need to remember, though, is that the answers will come if you ask the right questions."

That was the problem though. What was the right question? I climbed down off him, trying to figure out what I could possibly do to make it harder on him to stand still than it was to go forward.

After several minutes, it suddenly came to me. I was surprised I hadn't thought of it before. One of the hardest things for a horse to do is stand on three legs. They can do it, but not for long. It's extremely tiring for them even when they're standing still. I'd never tried it on a horse with this problem before, but figured, what the heck? It was worth a shot, and it might save this horse.

I went to the barn and brought back a cotton lead rope with a bull snap on it. Then I got back on and gave him one more chance to do the right thing, which was to move off with only light leg pressure. He didn't. I got off immediately and tied up one of his front legs. I made a one-leg hobble out of the lead rope by putting the end of the lead rope through the bull snap. I then took the loop made by the lead rope, brought the leg up, and put the rope around the horse's forearm and pastern. When I tightened the rope, it put the leg in a bind. I stood there next to him, holding the leg up and hoping this would work.

After three minutes, there was no difference. After five minutes, the muscles above the tied leg began to quiver. At seven minutes, he started to go down and was in a slight panic. I immediately let the leg down, rubbed it, and got back on. He had a completely different look to him. His head was up, he was alert, and his ears were on me. Finally, after an hour, I had gotten his attention.

I gave him a little leg, and he offered to step. The pressure came off at once. I gave him some more leg, and he gave me another try. I then gave him a little more light pressure. This time he took two steps. Again I let him rest and gave him a pat on the neck. I applied more leg, and finally we were off. He walked down the road as if nothing was or ever had been wrong. I was completely amazed that something so simple could have made such a big difference. It was hard to believe that removing the comfort of standing on four legs, even without my being on him, was enough to get him to think about moving forward.

Of course, that isn't to say that his problem was entirely over. During the next couple of weeks, it arose several more times. The difference was that I now had the key to motivate him to move, which was tying his leg up. The thing was, I never had to go that far again. Anytime he would balk, I would simply have to start going through the routine of light leg pressure, bumping his sides, rein slaps, and head movement. Someplace along in that routine, he would willingly begin to move.

I got off immediately and tied up one of his front legs.

As time went on, even the rein slaps and head movement were eliminated because he'd begin to move with either light leg pressure or light kicks. Within about forty-five days, he no longer bothered to balk at all, but rather became very responsive and a pleasure to ride.

Now, it's hard to say for sure how Red's problem got started. He may have found that if he stood in one spot long enough, whoever was trying to make him move would quit and he wouldn't have to work, or maybe he just wanted to be asked to move instead of being told or forced. Whatever his reasons, he'd now made up his mind that it was easier to move when asked than it was not to move.

As with any horse-training problem, it's a whole lot easier to stop the problem before it starts than it is to correct it after it has. This is especially true when dealing with horses that balk.

Of course, it also helps to have an idea of what is causing a balking problem before trying to fix it. The causes that I have run across have ranged from a sudden unfamiliar sight, sound, or smell, to fatigue or soreness. I have also seen horses balk because of a cinch that was too tight, tack that didn't fit properly, and poor or uneven footing. A young or green horse may balk occasionally because he's having trouble keeping his balance while carrying the weight of a rider on his back. To be honest, just about anything can cause the problem. The most common reason horses balk is because their riders have allowed them to or, in a sense, taught them to.

For instance, a horse that constantly balks at the arena gate usually does so because every time he's worked, that's where his rider dismounts when they are through. The horse naturally associates the gate with being able to stop and rest and will try to do so every time he gets near it. All a rider has to do to avoid teaching this to his horse is dismount in different areas of the arena when the session is through or exercise the horse after leaving the arena. In other words, don't allow the horse to consider the gate to be anything more than a place to enter and exit. It's as simple as that.

However, for a horse that balks as a matter of course, whether it be at a gate, out on the trail, or in any other situation, it's important to show him in a positive and meaningful way that what he's doing is not desirable behavior. The easiest way I've found to do that is to make it simply more work for him to stop than it is to go forward. I'm not talking about flogging the horse every time he stops, but rather putting him in a situation in which he is forced to use both his mind and his body in a way that is uncomfortable for him.

Not only do I use the techniques that I got from the old man, but for horses that aren't as serious about balking as others, I've also done things as simple as pulling the horse in a tight circle or asking him to back for fifteen or twenty feet. This is usually enough to cause him to decide against stopping simply because he wants to, which in turn, fixes the problem before it gets out of hand.

There's no question that a horse that constantly balks or stops for no reason can be more than just a little bit annoying. He can also be very dangerous, as I found out firsthand. Armed with the proper attitude, patience, and a little know how, you can fix even the most difficult balking problems in a relatively short time, without traumatizing either you or the horse.

The thing that is important to understand is that no two horses are exactly alike. What works on one may not work on another. It just makes sense that some balking problems are going to be easier to fix than others. There is one thing I always try to remember, though, especially when looking for quiet solutions to annoying and dangerous problems. That is, just like the old man said, the answers will come if you ask the right questions. The hard part is knowing the right questions to ask, and then taking the time to ask them.

NOTES FOR BALKING

More than providing the reader with any earth shattering techniques or methods of dealing with horses that balk, my main goal with this chapter was providing a situation in which I was forced to "think outside the box" in order to find a way to help a horse see other ways to do things. I've never had what you might call formal lessons in how to work with horses; so much of what I've learned and done over the years has come through a sort of fly-by-the-seat-of-one's-pants way of learning. The method I used in this chapter about Red is a by-product of that thinking.

Because I never really had anybody standing over my shoulder telling me something wasn't going to work when it came to working with horses, I discovered a freedom to try whatever I thought might fit the situation. As a result I've blindly stumbled upon things that some people might look at as relatively unconventional as far as ways of working with horses. The one leg hobble I used with Red was one of these. Interestingly, some of the things I've come up with (such as using the one leg hobble on a horse that balks) have ended up being so specific to the horse in question that I seldom had to use the method again. In fact, in the case of the one leg hobble, and other than Red, I only used that particular method on two other occasions in the past twenty years.

Stopping the unstoppable horse

There's one thing about training horses in the mountains that I've always looked at as sort of a hindrance. That is, it's nearly impossible to find a piece of ground that is naturally, totally flat. Everything, and I mean everything, sits at some sort of an angle. As a result, any training work that I do with horses is done with them going either straight up, straight down, or traversing the side of a hill. For the most part, this has always been a bit of an annoyance and something I've had to learn to live with. However, I do recall one horse where working in the mountains was not only beneficial to him, but also played a major part in solving a very dangerous and deep-rooted problem.

The horse was a twelve-year-old bay gelding named Jack that had lived most of his life as a barrel racer. His owner had decided to sell him, because he had not only become hard to stop, but was also no longer turning. In other words, he would run as fast as he could into the arena, then go right past the first barrel without even attempting to go around it, no matter how hard she tried to turn him.

The horse's new owner had visions of using him strictly as a pleasure and trail horse. Unfortunately, she quickly began to see that his many years of doing nothing but running any time someone was on his back had definitely taken its toll on him. Each time she got on him, all he wanted to do was run. After weeks of fruitless attempts to get him to walk while riding, she brought him to me to see if I could get him to slow down.

I tried to explain that horses that have lived their lives in a race environment are conditioned to do nothing else. As a result, it's often better for the horse to let him do what he does best, in this case, run races. I also tried to explain that trying to recondition this horse from a runner to a walker could be very time consuming. Not only that, but there was always the possibility that once he was reconditioned, he could revert back at any time. I suggested that perhaps her energy and money would be better spent with a horse that she wouldn't have to completely retrain, as she would have to do with this one.

She wouldn't hear of it. She had fallen in love with this horse and was more than willing to do whatever it was going to take to make him into the horse she wanted. So, with that, we started Jack's retraining.

At the time, I was working at a ranch at the foot of Twin Sisters Mountain. The ranch sits at an elevation of about 9,200 feet and was built entirely on a gradual, heavily wooded slope. Near the entrance to the ranch was a small, makeshift riding arena that measured about 50 by 100 feet. The arena was also built on a gradual slope. It was to this arena that we brought Jack and began his reconditioning.

I could tell as soon as I sat in the saddle for the first time and asked him to move off that I definitely had my work cut out for me. I had no sooner offered to put pressure on his sides to get some forward movement than he took off running like he'd been shot out of a gun. The power he used to take off was so intense that he nearly gave me whiplash. He traveled over forty feet at this high rate of speed before I even realized we weren't standing still anymore.

An attempt to slow him down by pulling back on the reins proved to be absolutely fruitless. I could quickly see that I would have had better luck trying to stop water from running downhill than I would have trying to stop this horse. Luckily, we were in the confines of the arena, which he seemed happy to stay within. Had we been in an open field somewhere, there's no telling where we might have ended up.

I decided that perhaps the best plan of attack with this horse would be simply to let him run until he played himself out. Then, when he was tired, I would again ask him to slow down. Hopefully by that time, he would be willing to listen and respond. Of course, I say this as if I had other options I could use. The truth of the matter is, I didn't. Because

I would have had better luck trying to stop water from running downhill.

he refused to stop or even slow down when I asked, I was pretty much at his mercy. All I could do was stay on and wait for him to tire out.

As we made lap after lap around the arena at speeds that I wasn't entirely comfortable with, I began to make an effort to do two things. The first was to avoid bumping or kicking him with my heels or legs, which he might have mistaken for me wanting him to go faster or continue at the pace he was already traveling. The second was to put my weight in awkward positions in the saddle, making it hard for him to carry. This, in turn, would also make it difficult for him to continue at the faster speed.

He ran for all he was worth for nearly ten minutes before I began to notice his movements becoming labored. He had worked himself into a lather and was breathing hard through his nose as his pace began to slow. As it did, I once again asked him to slow to a walk by picking up on the reins. This time, he responded. He came out of his fast lope and dropped into a trot that he remained in for another lap. Finally, he slowed to a walk. However, he remained in the walk only long enough to catch his breath. Then once again, he moved off into a lope.

We repeated this same process several more times within the next hour or so. In each case, I asked him to slow only after I knew that he was tired enough to want to respond. I also did absolutely nothing to encourage him to move faster than a walk. If he did move faster, he did so because he wanted to, not because I was asking him to. What I was trying to show him was that it was going to be a tremendous amount of work for him to do what he wanted to do, which was to go fast. If he did what I wanted him to do, which was to move at a walk, he didn't have to work nearly as hard. Hopefully once he understood that, he would decide on his own to start responding to the cues I was giving him.

After working with him for over an hour and a half, it became easy to see that he was completely exhausted. The good thing was that he was now very willing to respond to any and all cues that I gave him. Because he was responding so well, along with the fact that he was so tired he could hardly move, I decided to stop for the day.

It would take another four days of working with him in the same way before he wouldn't try to run off as soon as I sat down in the saddle. It was an additional week after that before I could actually get on and have him move off calmly in a walk.

From then on, he began to make progress in leaps and bounds. His attitude had changed completely, and he was becoming increasingly easier to control. Turning, stopping, and backing no longer required a major effort on my part.

I'd been working with him for nearly a month before finally deciding to take him out of the little arena and test his newfound abilities on the trail. I started the day by taking him down to the arena and riding around for about fifteen to twenty minutes. I did this to make sure that he was still responding to my cues, the same ones I would be using once we were on the trail. He was very quiet and responsive just as he had been for the past three weeks or so, and I was quite confident that he'd be a perfect gentleman out on the trail. So, with that, I dismounted, led him out of the arena and got back on. Almost immediately I could feel his body tense up in a way that I hadn't felt since the first day I rode him.

In an attempt to try to settle him down, I slowly reached down and gave him a gentle pat on the neck. Unfortunately, he apparently mistook the shifting of my weight as a request on my part to take off running as fast as he could, which he did. I tried three or four times to ask him to slow down by pulling back on the reins, but just like the first day, there was no response. It didn't take long for me to realize that if I was going to survive this stampede, I'd have to do a couple of things.

The first and most obvious thing was to stay on his back. If I fell off at the speed we were traveling while passing over the countless rocks and moving through lodgepole pine, there was no question that I'd be in pretty rough shape by the time I stopped. The second thing I needed to do was keep him headed uphill. This would certainly take the wind out of his sails quicker than if he were on the flat or going downhill.

Keeping him headed uphill was not at all difficult, seeing how that was the direction he was headed when he took off running. That, coupled with the fact that he was refusing to respond to any request I made to either stop or turn, made it pretty safe that we were going to stay in a straight line. Luckily that line was uphill and straight up the ranch driveway, which led to its main buildings.

Towards the top, the driveway branched off in a "Y" intersection. To the right lay the main buildings of the ranch. To the left was an old logging road that continued uphill and became even steeper the higher it went. As we reached the intersection, I pulled the horse off to the left, continuing uphill, which he seemed more than happy to do. However, as we continued upward and Jack began to tire, he decided to get off the road and start heading through the trees. This concerned me because, as I said earlier, the forest in the area was quite thick. As a result, there was barely enough room for the horse to squeeze between the trees himself, let alone with someone on his back.

Fortunately, by the time he headed into the trees, he had already lost most of his steam and all of his enthusiasm about continuing. This still wasn't enough to make him want to come to a complete stop. As he continued, I was forced to duck under low-hanging branches and lift my knees clear up the pommel of the saddle to avoid rapping them on trees as we passed.

Finally, we came to a clearing about twenty feet in diameter. As we entered it, I pulled Jack to a stop, which he did very willingly. He appeared to be completely exhausted as he stood with his head low, taking deep labored breaths, with beads of sweat dripping off him. We stood just long enough for his breathing to become a little less labored. I then turned and headed him back downhill. We went only a short distance before running into another narrow logging road. The road that had brought us up the hill ran east and west. This one, in contrast, went north and south, traversing the hill, and was relatively flat. I decided to stay on this road for a while to let him relax and cool off before continuing back down the hill.

Much to my surprise, after only a few minutes, he again seemed to be building up energy. His walk became stiff as he began leaning on the bit and tossing his head. He also began to blow hard through his nose from time to time as if he were protesting the speed at which we were traveling.

Then, just as suddenly as before, he exploded and took off running for all he was worth. Immediately I turned him uphill into the trees. Luckily we were in a spot where the trees weren't as thick, so dodging them, for me, was easier. The grade that we were on was also steeper, which made him fight for every step. He went only about two hundred yards this time before coming to a stop on his own. Now there was no question that he'd used up every bit of energy he had.

He stood on the side of the hill trembling both from fighting to catch his breath and from trying to hold up my weight as well as his. I let him stand for a few minutes before asking him to move forward. He couldn't. If he had tried to take a step with me on him, he surely would have fallen. Seeing this, I slowly climbed down off of him. This movement was enough to pull him off balance to the point where his knees actually buckled. I loosened his cinch and let him stand for a few more minutes before leading him back down the hill and heading for the barn.

Jack had evidently decided that his last trip up the hill was one trip too many. It had made a big enough impression on him that he never again tried to run off. Looking back, I think that had I not had the advantage of his running uphill at an altitude of 9,200 feet, this may not have been possible. Using the same technique on the same horse in a large flat area wouldn't have had the same impact on him. He was simply too strong, had too much energy, and recovered too quickly. He may have looked at something like that as more of a game than a lesson to be learned.

Of course, not all horses with similar problems are as bad off as Jack was. For instance, I recall another horse that had trouble stopping when asked, and with him I used a completely different method. The horse, a young paint gelding, had become hard to stop due mainly to the bit used by his previous trainer. The trainer, who had been under pressure by the horse's owner to develop a more responsive stop in the animal, had taken him out of the D-ring snaffle bit that he'd been started in and put him in a more severe twisted-wire snaffle.

Now, a twisted-wire snaffle is just that. A snaffle bit made out of two or three pieces of heavy wire, usually copper, that have been twisted together. To say the least, it's certainly not the most comfortable bit for a horse, especially a young horse with a sensitive mouth.

I should take a minute here and clear up a common misconception concerning the sensitivity of a young or unbroke horse's mouth. Many people think that a horse that has never had a bit in his mouth hasn't had a chance to develop a "hard" mouth and should automatically be ultra-responsive. To an extent, that is true. The catch is that while the horse's mouth is indeed very sensitive, it is a sensitivity that has to be developed. What I mean by this is that we, as trainers, have a very clear picture in our heads as to what we want the horse to do and what it takes to get the horse to do it. Take stopping, for instance. We know that to get a stop, all we have to do is pull back on the reins. Simple as that. For a horse that knows what the cue means, the response is easy. However, for a horse that doesn't know what it means, the cue is simply a source of confusion. In his confusion, the horse may do things that a rider could mistake as him being "hard-mouthed." He may pull or lean on the bit. He may also toss or shake his head or simply walk or run right through the pressure.

For a young horse, there's one other thing that often compounds these problems. That is the fact that he may still be trying to learn how to walk while carrying the weight of a person on his back. Believe it or not, that is also something that a horse has to be taught. A horse that is having trouble carrying weight will often lean heavily on the bit, using it as sort of a fifth leg to help him keep his balance. For someone who overlooks these things or who simply regards them as the horse being belligerent or hard to get along with, problems such as the horse becoming hard to stop are sure to come along.

From what I was able to pick up from the little paint gelding, my guess was that his problems had stemmed from this type of misunderstanding. Instead of trying to work through the horse's problem, his trainer simply decided that the easy way to fix him was to put him in a more severe bit. Well, the trainer was wrong. Unfortunately, it did nothing to fix the problem and in some ways made things even worse.

By the time the gelding came to me, he was in pretty bad shape. Not only did he not stop, but he was also very forceful about pushing through any pressure that was applied to the bit. I felt that working with him in a large area where he could possibly get up a big head of steam might be a mistake. So I decided that, at least for the first few sessions, I would work him in the small confines of a thirty-foot round pen. I also replaced the twisted-wire snaffle bit (which obviously wasn't working for him) with the normal snaffle that he had been started in.

I was fairly certain that the reason he had become so hard to stop was that the twisted-wire bit had been causing him so much pain that he simply felt the need to defend himself. As a result, instead of giving to its pressure and stopping, he would do just the opposite and push against it. This is really a very normal and surprisingly common reaction and is the biggest reason horses become hard-mouthed to begin with. The good thing is it's usually easily fixed.

This gelding appeared to be very quiet as we entered the round pen and I climbed on him for the first time. He was also very responsive as I gave him a little leg, asking him to move forward. Not wanting him to get too much forward momentum, we had gone only a short distance before I lightly picked up the reins and asked him to stop. He responded by sticking his nose out and walking right through the pressure.

I asked him to stop three more times with the same result, before finally taking the slack out of the right rein and pulling his head to the inside. This forced him into a very tight and uncomfortable circle. He circled about a half dozen times before finally coming to a stop. As he did, I let him have his head back and let him stand for a few seconds before again picking up the reins, this time to ask him to back.

One of the things that I have come to understand over the years is that, as a rule, if a horse doesn't know how to back on cue, chances are he won't stop on cue. By the same token, if he backs well, he will more than likely stop well. This horse did neither. I decided that perhaps the best way to teach this horse how to stop was first to teach him to back.

I have a very simple and methodical way of doing this. First, I shift my weight backwards in the saddle. This gives the horse the idea of which direction I'm going to ask him to go even before I ask. Second, I take just enough slack out of the reins so that there is a slight backward pressure on the bit. I then anchor my hands, usually to the saddle, so that my hands aren't constantly moving and the pressure stays consistent.

With this pressure on the horse's mouth, he soon begins to look for a way to get rid of it. His first option is usually to lean into it. When that doesn't work, he may toss his head from side to side or up and down. He may also try a couple of other meaningless options before finally trying to move backwards.

This horse's backward try was nothing more than a slight shift of his weight in that direction. Still, it was enough to warrant a reward from me, which was an immediate release of the pressure and a couple of pats on the neck. I let him stand for a few seconds before again shifting my weight back, taking the slack out of the reins, and setting my

He was willingly taking about eight to ten steps backwards.

hands. This time he responded almost immediately with a bigger shift of his weight. Again I rewarded him.

In less than five minutes, he was willingly taking about eight to ten steps backwards with a very light pressure from me. Within about fifteen minutes, he would begin to back as soon as I shifted my weight in that direction. Within twenty minutes, he would back clear across the round pen without stopping. At that point, it was finally time to ask him to go forward and stop on cue.

Now again, the last thing I wanted was for him to get up too much forward momentum, which would make it harder for him to stop. So, as I asked him to go forward, it was only for about three steps before I leaned back in the saddle and picked up the reins. He stopped so quickly that you would have thought that somebody had glued his feet to the ground. I immediately released the pressure, let him stand for a few seconds, then asked him to back, which he did without hesitation.

From that point on, each time I asked him to stop, I also asked him to back. I did this so that he would automatically associate stopping with going backwards. In other words, each time he was asked to stop he would be thinking "back." This, in turn, would make his stops more fluid. It also made the whole stopping process easier for him to understand and perform.

I continued working with the horse in the same manner for the next two weeks. Each time I rode him, I not only increased the distance he moved before asking him to stop, but as time went on, I also increased the speed at which we were traveling. By the end of the two weeks, he could not only be stopped dead out of a fast lope, but he would also willingly regulate his speed with the mere shifting of my weight. A shift of weight forward would speed him up. A shift backwards would slow him down.

In fact, the horse had become so responsive and well mannered that his owner, a young pharmacist, decided to enter him in an open horse show about a month later. Surprisingly enough, the little gelding ended up bringing home two first-place ribbons and one second place. His owner was so happy with his performance at that show that the two of them spent nearly every weekend that summer on the local show circuit and had a ball doing it.

———

Even with successes such as this, I must admit that working with horses that don't want to stop is not one of my most favorite things to do. To be honest, working with one that is real adamant about not stopping can be both frightening and dangerous and is not something that I ever look forward to doing.

I guess the reason is that I have seen, firsthand, the damage that a serious runaway can cause to both horse and rider. I know of people who have suffered broken backs and fractured skulls because a horse that they couldn't get pulled up ran into a wall or fence. I even know of one case where a lady was killed when the horse she was riding ran out of control into the fast-moving traffic of a nearby highway.

Frankly, I never could understand why anybody would ever want to own a horse that he or she couldn't stop or at least get slowed down in that type of circumstance. By the same token, I realize that just about any horse, under a highly stressful situation, is capable of becoming terribly frightened and stampeding off. However, in about ninety percent of the cases where a horse runs off with a rider because he's frightened, it is the rider's inability to think and act clearly that gets them both in trouble.

Most riders, when faced with a situation in which the horse they are riding suddenly panics and runs off, all do one thing. They pull straight back on the reins with all their might, trying to get the horse to stop. Unfortunately, for a horse in a panic situation, that is usually the worst thing they could do.

The thing we have to remember is that a truly frightened horse will be forced to run away from that which has frightened it. He has no choice. It is his instinct that is controlling him. Because his instinct is telling him to run away, it only makes sense that he is not going to want to be held back or confined while doing it. By pulling directly back on the reins, we are doing just that, trying to confine him. At least that's how he sees it.

Because we are trying to confine him, he is naturally going to fight harder to get away in order to save himself. To compound the problem, the rider of an out-of-control horse naturally begins to panic as well. The horse senses that the rider is now frightened, which only serves to reinforce in his mind the reason why he panicked to begin with. The horse and rider feed off each other's fear until the next thing they know, they end up in Idaho stampeding through a potato patch.

By understanding what the horse is thinking and going through in a situation like this, we can then make a rational decision on how to bring him back under control. What I usually do is take one rein and pull the horse's head off to one side or the other, forcing him into a tight circle. If I catch him soon enough into the panic, he will simply circle right there in that spot. He'll go around a few times, expending the energy that his flight instinct is forcing him to use, before finally coming to a stop and trying to get a look at what it was that frightened him.

If I don't catch him soon enough and he starts running away, I still do the same thing, take one rein and pull his head off to the side. This allows him to get away, but because his head is off to the side, it throws him off balance. This not only makes running physically difficult for him, but also allows him to expend his energy in a relatively controlled manner. The rider having control in a situation like this is usually the difference between having a serious wreck and getting out of the mess unscathed.

Now I'm certainly not trying to say that this will work on 100 percent of all runaway horses, because it won't. There are some runaways that are just too enthusiastic. (It is those horses, by the way, that I would rather not even bother throwing a leg over because they are flat out too dangerous.) Rather, this is a method that will usually work on young, inexperienced horses that are looking for direction and older, trustworthy horses that have become frightened because of seeing or hearing something out of the ordinary.

It has also been my experience that the best way to overcome a problem like this is not to allow it to happen in the first place. In other words, by teaching your horse how to stop properly to begin with, along with making sure that he has confidence that you will help him through scary situations, running away or being hard to stop will simply not be an option for him.

I'm sure for some folks these things may sound easier said than done. To be honest, for some folks, they are. However, there is one thing I do know and that is that most horses will go out of their way to try to be dependable for you. The problem is, before that can happen, they first have to be able to depend on you.

All it really takes to develop that kind of trust is three little things: time, patience, and understanding. It's the people who don't take the time to do things right, don't have the patience to help the animal instead of force him, or don't try to understand his point of view, who run into trouble. It's also those same people who usually end up stampeding through Idaho potato patches on out-of-control horses wondering why they can't get their dang horse to stop.

Well, now we know.

NOTES FOR STOPPING THE UNSTOPPABLE HORSE

This is one of the only chapters in the book where my thoughts on the subject, as well as the methods I used back when I wrote it, haven't varied too much from what I do today. I still use the idea of backing to teach a horse how to soften and give to the bit rather than push or brace against it. I also still stress the idea of using pressure without pulling, although through my work in martial arts I feel I have greatly refined the way I teach it to both riders as well as horses. For instance, I seldom, if ever use the idea of anchoring the reins to the pommel of the saddle anymore. Instead, I rely more on what I refer to as a "live" connection between the horse and myself through the reins to communicate what I'm looking for. When working with a student, I also spend time working with their hands to teach them the feel of this "live" connection, so they can in turn pass it on to their horse.

Like so many other things in the way I work with horses these days, I'm much more apt to direct a horse that is having trouble stopping than I am to let them run, as I described in the chapter with Jack. What I mean when I say "directing" is simply giving the horse some guidance after the request (if the horse doesn't stop) such as circling or doing small figure eights or serpentines until they offer to stop, or at the very least, offer to change their speed. In other words, I try to offer the horse something that causes them to have to think back to the rider instead of simply charging into the bit.

One other thing that I have made a conscious effort to change over the years has to do with the way I ride overall, but in particular it has to do with something I mentioned in the way I used to ask a horse to go backwards. In the chapter I spoke about how, when asking the horse to back up, that I shifted my weight slightly backward in the saddle to help the horse understand that is the direction we are getting ready to go. Over the years (and again, primarily due to my training in martial arts) I have gotten away from doing anything in the saddle that may take me out of balance. As a result, I have almost completely gotten away from obvious shifts of weight, leaning forward or back in the saddle, pushing my feet in the stirrups, and anything else that may either cause a brace in my body or take me or the horse out of balance.

Not having to deal with an out of balance or stiff rider can make the horse's job easier and can go a long way to resolving most riding issues.

Head tossing

As I remember, it had been snowing for about two hours that Saturday morning. Luckily, it wasn't the type of snow that was going to stick on the ground and turn everything white. The reason being was that it was mid-April, and winter had long since disappeared, with the last real storm taking place nearly two months earlier. In fact, it had been so warm during the past three weeks that the ground had not only thawed out completely, but it wasn't even that wet. It was those warm, sunny days that had been instrumental in drying the normally saturated ground. As a result, the place had taken on the look and feel of midsummer instead of early spring.

So, the wet snow that was falling that day melted almost as soon as it hit the ground, which turned the area around the barn into a greasy, muddy mess. It was a firm reminder that, as much as it may have felt like summer, it wasn't really here yet.

As I walked into the tack room, making sure to stomp as much of the mud off my boots as I could, I noticed the old man sitting quietly in his favorite chair repairing a broken bridle and puffing on an ever-present cigarette.

"Think it might snow today?" he questioned jokingly, without bothering to look up.

"It might," I replied, with a smile.

"Got your chores done?"

"Yup," I nodded. "All I have left is to check the water tank out in the pasture."

"Good," he said, flatly. "When you're done with that, come on back. I've got a horse I need you to try out."

"Is it that sorrel I saw in the foaling stall?"

"Yeah," he said, as the long piece of gray ash that had been dangling on the end of his cigarette dropped off, landing harmlessly in his lap. "She came in yesterday, and I haven't had a chance to see what she knows."

"Okay," I told him. "I'll be right back."

By the time I got out to the pasture, filled the water tank, and returned to the barn, the old man had already bridled and saddled the horse and was making his way out to the little makeshift round pen he had set up in a grassy field near the hay barn. It was about the only spot on the whole place that wasn't covered with mud.

"I don't know a thing about her," the old man said, as I swung up into the saddle, "so make sure you go slow with her. I don't want no wrecks today."

"I don't want one either," I said, as I gently picked up the reins and softly applied a little leg, asking the horse to move forward.

She responded without hesitation and appeared quite comfortable as we made our way to the rail and walked in circles around the old man, who stayed in the middle of the pen. We had made about three trips around the inside of the pen before the old man asked me to bring the horse off the rail and head in the opposite direction. As I gently started to take the slack out of the inside rein to turn the horse, I noticed that she began to toss her head in the air. When the turn was completed, the head tossing stopped. We went only one lap when the old man asked me to reverse direction once more. As I did, the head tossing started again and quit when the turn was completed.

"We need to see something here," the old man said, lighting up another cigarette. "Go ahead and ask her to stop, but be careful. She may want to toss her head when you do."

"Okay," I said, with confidence. After all, even if she did toss her head, what harm could she possibly do to me?

174

She threw her head up so hard and so fast that I never even saw it coming.

With that, I picked up on the reins and asked her to come to a stop. Just that fast, I came to realize what kind of harm a head tosser could cause. She threw her head up so hard and so fast that I really never even saw it coming. The one thing I do remember seeing, though, just before her head collided with mine, was her nose sticking almost straight up in the air. I remember thinking that that was a strange angle for her nose to be at, just before my lights went out.

The impact of her head hitting my face was so great that she literally launched me out of the saddle and over her back end, landing me unceremoniously on my head in the wet grass. The impact damaged one of my front teeth, which in later years would force me to have a root canal done on it. To this day, that tooth is still pushed slightly out of place.

"Guess she's a bit of a head tosser," I heard the old man say from his position in the middle of the pen, as I tried to shake the cobwebs from my head. "You okay? That looked like it hurt." It did, but I wasn't about to tell him that.

That was the very first time I rode or worked with a horse that was a head tosser, and she is the one horse that always pops into my head each time I've worked with one since. At the time, all I could think of was how mad I was that the mare had loosened my tooth and busted my lip. Now I'm a little more forgiving, because I understand what causes a horse to become a head tosser and what it takes to fix the problem.

You see, more times than not, head tossing is caused by a miscommunication between horse and rider during the stages of the horse's early training. I'm talking specifically of a young horse's lack of understanding of the bit.

Often what happens is that a colt is expected to stop by giving to pressure from the bit. Not understanding what this pressure means, the colt begins to search for a way to relieve himself of it. During this search, he will try several different options. The options include leaning on the bit, shaking his head from side to side, opening his mouth as wide as it will go, or laying his head on his chest, before he finally gives to the pressure by stopping or backing.

Head tossing usually begins when either too much pressure is applied or when no relief is given for a proper response on the horse's part. The head tossing often becomes worse when the rider, trying to stop the horse from throwing his head, mistakenly begins to increase the amount of pressure applied.

The rider may also make the common mistake of blaming the bit for the problem. In a case like that, I have seen riders go through any number of different bits in search of one that they feel the horse will be comfortable with. Usually they end up settling on a mechanical hackamore, often coupled with a tie-down. Other riders, while looking for the most stopping power they can muster, may simply use the most severe bit they can find and couple this with a tie-down made from chain or cable. Unfortunately, both of these options only serve to treat the symptoms and do nothing to solve the problem. In fact, they often have the opposite effect; they compound the problem.

Obviously, the best way to cure a horse of tossing his head is stopping him before he starts. In other words, being more sensitive to his reactions to the cues given to him in the early stages of his training. However, it has been my observation that most horse owners acquire head tossers long after the damage of their early years has been done by trainers or the original owner. Because of the varying degrees of severity of the problem, trying to fix a head-tossing problem can many times be as frustrating as the problem itself, especially for the novice horse owner.

I have found that most average head tossers have one thing in common. That is that they don't give well to pressure. They often don't stop very readily, nor do they give to lateral pressure. In order to help the animal understand that there is no need for him to throw his head, he must first learn to give to this pressure.

Because most head tossers associate throwing their heads with having someone on their backs, I like to do the first stages of my corrective process from the ground. This sometimes limits the need for the horse to feel like he has to toss his head initially and also gives him more time to concentrate on what we're doing.

I always begin by having the horse saddled and in a snaffle bit. I then gently ask him to give his head laterally by slowly drawing the rein back to the saddle. During this time, I try to take special care to relieve the horse of any pressure I'm applying as soon as he offers to give to it, thereby reinforcing the proper response. If he begins to fight or push against the bit, I try to anchor the rein to his neck, mane, or the saddle until he quits fighting. I then let him rest before continuing.

On occasion I run across a horse that has no intention of cooperating with me. This was the case with a big, black quarter horse named Star. Star had been a head tosser for quite some time and was actually very good at it. Each time I asked for his head, he continuously fought and tried to pull away. When he finally did give in to the pressure and I in turn gave him some relief, he defiantly took his head back. In a case like his, I usually take one rein, run it under the opposite pommel swell of the saddle, then over the seat and back to the side where I'm standing. Then I turn the horse's head towards me, holding it there with the rein until he finds the proper way to relieve himself of the pressure, which is simply to give to it. I repeat this on both sides until he willingly bends to light lateral pressure.

Now, some people use a short cut when asking a "sour" horse to bend in such a way. They do this by tying the horse's head back to the saddle, forcing him to figure out what the right thing is.

I'm not a believer in that method for a couple of reasons. First, by working the rein manually instead of tying it, I can give the horse a more immediate reward (releasing the pressure), if it is warranted. Second, if the horse begins to fight the pressure to the point where he could hurt himself, I can simply let go of the rein so he can get away from it. If he is tied, damage could be done before I get a chance to untie him.

Star was not a very willing participant in learning how to give to lateral pressure and fought like crazy any time I asked him to. If I asked him to turn to the left, he'd pull to the right. If I asked him to go right, he'd pull left. The one good thing about running the rein under the pommel of the saddle, as I was forced to do with him, is that the leather rein against the leather saddle allows very little slippage, no matter how hard a horse pulls in an attempt to get away. As a result, the horse can fight as hard as he wants, but as long as he doesn't jerk the rein out of my hand, he won't be able to avoid the pressure.

I must admit, Star was very innovative in his attempts to avoid doing what was being asked of him. He tried everything from throwing his head and then holding it high in the air, to pushing his nose as close to the ground as he could. He would then lean into the pressure to the point where I felt had I let go of the rein, he might actually have fallen over.

It had taken nearly twenty minutes of working with him before he finally quit fighting long enough to try to give to the pressure. When he did, he inadvertently rewarded himself by causing slack to develop in the rein. Once he did that, it was as if a light went on in his head, and almost immediately he quit fighting altogether. Less than five minutes after the first time he gave to the pressure, he decided willingly to turn his head to the left when I used only light pressure on the rein. Unfortunately, it took nearly another twenty minutes for him to learn the same thing on the right side. Because it had taken him so long to learn this one simple thing and because he was now doing it so well, I decided to quit for the day. Quitting on a positive note is important for both the horse and the person working with him.

When we started up the next day, we did so by reinforcing everything he had done to that point, which was simply giving laterally in both directions with me standing on the ground. He was doing that very nicely in less than five minutes, so it was time to take the next step. That was to get on and start working on the head-tossing problem itself.

Once on his back, I again asked him to lightly give his head first to the left, then to the right. He hesitated slightly in both directions, but then gave to the pressure as nicely as he had with me standing on the ground. With that, the work on his actual problem began.

I usually take one rein and run it under the opposite pommel swell.

Using only light, two-handed pressure, I picked up the reins and asked him to think about moving backwards. This is usually all it takes to get a horse with this type of problem to start tossing his head to one degree or another.

I have found that if the horse is not a very severe head tosser, sometimes all it takes to get him to stop is taking the slack out of the reins and anchoring my hands to the pommel of the saddle. By anchoring the reins in such a way, each time he tosses his head, he finds the parameters that I'm asking him to use. If his head leaves those parameters, he causes himself undue discomfort by hitting the bit. Soon, he figures out that he can relieve himself of this discomfort by holding his head in one place. Only then can we continue to ask him to back.

Unfortunately, Star did not fit into that category. Instead, he was what I consider a severe head tosser. This is the type of horse whose problem has become so bad that even the lightest pressure on the bit causes a violent and potentially dangerous head tossing incident. In the most severe cases, the horse may actually rear or offer to rear as he tosses his head. Luckily, Star wasn't quite that bad yet. I'll tell you one thing, though. He wasn't far from it.

I had no sooner begun applying the light backwards pressure than he immediately thrust his head forward. He did so with such force that he literally pulled me out of the saddle. This, in turn, left me no alternative but to pull back on him, just so I could regain my balance. It's this type of seesaw pulling match that has to be avoided if any progress is going to be made in fixing this problem. The thing is, that usually with a severe head tosser, the longer you hold the reins, no matter how light the pressure, the more violent the horse becomes. He not only will continue to thrust his head forward, trying to get the reins out of your hands, but will also vigorously shake and toss his head.

While Star was doing this with me, I felt it was imperative that I, first, get his attention on me and, second, get him to stop acting up long enough to start thinking about the cues I was trying to give him. This is where the lateral control came into play.

As he fought, I took the left rein and brought his head around to the left side. Then I anchored the rein to my leg with my hand. This not only caused him to stop throwing his head, but also made it next to impossible for him to rear had he decided to do so. The other thing it caused him to do was begin circling. I tried to make these circles as tight and uncomfortable as possible for him, and let him do it for as long as he liked, which was about eight revolutions. As soon as he offered to stop circling, I began to give him his head back. When he finally came to a complete stop, I let him stand quietly for a few seconds before once again gently picking up the reins and applying light backwards pressure. He immediately began acting up. As he did, I quickly pulled his head off to the side, this time to the right, forcing him into more tight and uncomfortable circles.

We repeated this circling process each time he tried to toss his head or fight the light backward pressure that I was asking him to give to. It took nearly forty minutes of doing this before he finally stopped fighting.

I should point out here that I was not circling this horse as a punishment for doing something wrong. Instead I was trying to make a point. The point was that I needed his attention on me. If he was constantly fighting or tossing his head, there was no way that he could possibly pay attention to the business at hand. At the same time, I also wanted to try to show him that there was no longer a need for him to throw his head. If he did, he went to work. If he didn't, he got to stand quietly.

The reason I make this point is that some people rely entirely too much on circling their horses as a form of punishment instead of as a training tool. When this happens, both horse and rider lose track of why they're circling. This usually ends up causing additional problems for both of them, especially the horse, which may become belligerent and unresponsive.

Only after Star had quit fighting and I was fairly confident that he was willing to pay attention to the cues I was giving, did I start asking him to back again. It had become painfully obvious to me that the reason this horse had become a head tosser was that he simply had never been taught properly how to give to pressure from the bit. This is usually the problem with head tossers. That is why I feel that teaching this type of horse to back is so important. Clearly, if the horse backs well, he understands how to give to pressure. If he understands giving to pressure instead of fighting it, he'll no longer feel the need to toss his head.

Now, the way I teach this type of horse to back is almost identical to the way I teach a hard-to-stop horse how to back. I use light constant pressure, don't pull on his mouth, and reward even the smallest try. Even a halfhearted shift of his weight warrants a reward, even if the shift is by accident, which was the case with Star. As I was applying this light pressure, he picked up a foot to stomp at a fly and accidentally moved backwards. Still, I rewarded him for it by completely releasing the pressure and petting him while letting him stand quietly.

That was enough to get the ball rolling. The next time I picked up the reins, he made a bigger offer and received the same reward from me. Again I picked up the reins, and again he made an effort to respond. We continued to work this way for about the next fifteen minutes. By that time, he was willingly taking about four steps backwards using only one light cue.

Only when he was backing these short distances willingly and without tossing his head, did I allow him to move forward. I only wanted him to move a few steps at a time before I asked him to stop. That way he didn't generate too much forward momentum, which would have made stopping more difficult for him. When I asked him to stop, it was with the same amount of pressure that I'd been using when asking him to back. If he offered to stop without tossing his head, I immediately released the pressure, gave him a moment to rest and think about it, then asked him to back again. From then on, for the most part, each time I asked him to stop, I also asked him to back. That way, when I asked him to stop, he began thinking "back." Because he was anticipating backing, he began to use his head-tossing energy to prepare himself to step backwards.

When he was stopping and backing at short distances without tossing his head, I increased the distance that he moved forward before asking him to stop. When this appeared to be causing him little or no problem, I moved up into the faster gaits, working extensively in the walk and trot before asking for the lope.

After working with Star for over two weeks in the same consistent manner, we had all but eliminated his head-tossing problem. He had also developed such a powerful and responsive stop that the first time his owner asked him to stop out of a lope, he actually pitched her up onto his neck.

Now, while Star's problem started out as being pretty serious, at least it was fixable, because it was mostly just a training problem. I have worked with other horses with similar symptoms that weren't as easy to fix, because the problem stemmed more from ill-fitting tack, unseen sores, or mouth, tooth, or tongue problems. I have also known horses to have these symptoms because of back or leg ailments that had been causing discomfort. Of course, all of those types of things would always need to be corrected before even attempting to fix the head-tossing problem.

I have also come to understand that while head tossing may be a response that the horse has been taught by accident, if left unchecked, it may also become a terribly bad habit that will be difficult to break. It is for that reason that, while working with head toss-ers, I constantly have to remind myself to be patient, even more patient than usual. After all, this is usually a response that has developed over a number of years and is not neces-sarily one that is going to be fixed overnight. Even so, as with most any type of training problem, by using a little time, patience, and understanding, even a problem as irritating and potentially dangerous as head tossing can almost surely be brought under control. That way the chances of having a front tooth knocked loose from being hit in the face while riding are not only greatly reduced, but can be eliminated altogether. Take it from me, getting hit in such a way isn't near as much fun as it sounds, and for my money, should be avoided at all costs.

NOTES ON HEAD TOSSING

As with so many other "problem" behaviors that horses develop, my main concern these days is trying to find out why the issue started in the first place, and then dealing with it accordingly from there. Head tossing is definitely one of those issues. While the vast majority of horses have developed a head tossing issue due to a rider releasing pressure at the wrong time, many others toss their heads due to pain issues in their neck, back, and withers; teeth problems; bit issues including a low pallet (the roof of the mouth) or thick tongue or both; ill-fitting tack; unbalanced feet; bugs and/or flies irritating the eyes; and even eye or visual problems.

The solutions I spoke about in this chapter, like the ones I talked about in the chapter on Mounting Problems, have to do with dealing with a horse after they have already offered the behavior. However, these days before I work with any horse that tosses its head, I always check to see if there might be an outside issue, like one of those I mentioned above, causing the problem in the first place. Like so many other problem behaviors, by eliminating the outside source of the irritant, the problem often goes away on its own. Only if I'm convinced there is no outside cause do I then look at it from a training standpoint.

Most head tossing behavior not caused by an outside source usually stems from the rider releasing pressure at the wrong time. For instance, the rider might ask the horse to stop, which the horse does. However, along with the stop, the horse may also lean into the bit or even jerk down into the pressure. Even though the horse may be offering a brace or stiffness in the stop, the rider inadvertently releases, and before long the small lean or jerk on the bit the horse offered begins to escalate into the horse tossing its head. Often in cases like that, doing something as simple as holding the pressure (stabilizing the rein, but not pulling) until the horse softens is enough to make the horse start searching for a different, and more beneficial behavior.

As with all training . . . it's the release that teaches, whether we know we are releasing or not!

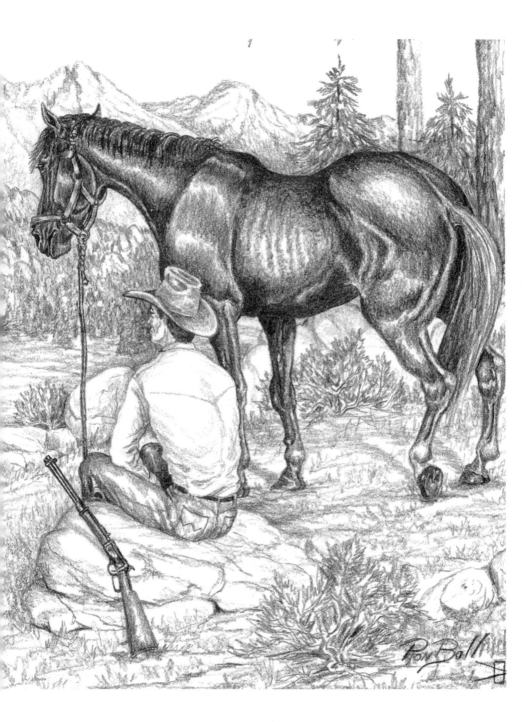

Seeing the teacher

Other than his name, which was Doc, and that at some point during his life he had dislocated his right hip, I didn't really know much about the old horse. The injury had been so severe that he'd been crippled ever since, with the range of motion in his right rear leg less than half of what it should have been. As a result, he always walked with a terrible limp. I wasn't even sure how old he was, although an educated guess would probably have put him somewhere between twenty-seven and thirty-two years.

I suppose the reason I didn't pay more attention to him was because I never had to take care of him. The old man did that. He not only fed and watered him, but also cleaned his pen on a daily basis, groomed him occasionally, and turned him out to pasture for an hour or so at a time, three or four times a week. I always thought doing that was a real nice gesture on the old man's part. It was clear that the only reason he did it at all was to break the monotony of the horse's day, because even though he was standing in knee-deep grass while in pasture, Doc's teeth were so bad he could no longer graze properly. He could pick the grass off with his front teeth but couldn't chew it. As a result, all the grass he tried to eat would simply ball up inside his mouth and drop out on the ground each time he opened it to get another bite.

Because he could no longer eat grass or hay of any kind, each day like clockwork the old man would go out and mix up a disgusting-looking, wet, mash-like substance in a bucket and feed it to Doc. I'm not sure what was in the mash, but whatever it was, it had kept the horse not only alive, but also fat and happy for at least two years.

The old man never spoke about the horse, nor did he ever complain about all the extra work that the horse caused him. The horse simply appeared to have become part of the old man's daily routine, like putting on his boots or lighting up his first cigarette of the morning.

The first time I recall even giving the horse a second look was one day as I was bringing a horse in off the pasture that was next to the pasture where Doc had been turned out. There was a large cottonwood tree near the fence, and Doc was standing quietly in its shade, lazily swishing his tail back and forth in a feeble attempt at keeping the ever-present flies off of his backside. For the first time in the two years since I'd first seen the horse, I thought that he appeared to be losing weight. I also thought that his normally shiny, bay-colored coat didn't seem to glow as it usually did.

When I got back to the barn, I asked the old man, almost as an afterthought, if Doc had, in fact, lost some weight.

"Maybe a little," he replied, quietly. "But I don't think it's anything to worry about."

"Oh, I'm not worried," I said, "just curious."

Looking back, I don't think it was me he was trying to convince, but rather himself, that nothing was wrong with the old horse. Unfortunately, as it turned out, there was indeed something to be worried about.

As the weeks passed, Doc lost more and more weight. He also appeared to be having a harder time getting around. The old hip injury, which had always hampered his movement, now appeared to be causing him an awful lot of pain, which it had never really done before.

Two-and-a-half months later, Doc had become a pitiful sight. Because of the pain in his hip, he now limited his own movement inside his pen to trips to his water tank and feed bucket. When the old man turned him out to pasture, he would walk ever-so-slowly out to the cottonwood tree and stand in the shade until the old man went back out to get him. He had also lost so much weight that he looked like little more than a skeleton with hide hanging on it, and all attempts to try to get more weight on him had failed miserably.

It was one day during this time that I came to work and noticed the old man out under the cottonwood tree. He was slowly digging what appeared to be a long, deep pit. I went out to see if he needed any help but his only reply was, "No, thanks. You've got work to do at the barn."

He worked on the pit for three days by himself. He alternated his digging with chopping through the cottonwood's massive outstretched roots with an ax. By the time he finished, the pit measured 4-feet wide, 10-feet long, and 8-feet deep.

The day after he finished the pit, he came to me with a lead rope in his hand.

"Here," he said, handing me the lead rope. "Go catch up Doc and take him out to the tree in the pasture." He paused. "I'll meet you out there."

I must have had a puzzled look on my face, because he automatically repeated himself in a quiet and reassuring tone. I entered Doc's pen, and he stood patiently waiting for me to approach. The old man didn't give me a halter for him and he wasn't wearing one, so I simply slid the rope over his neck and led him out to the pasture.

I had kind of a weird feeling as I walked with him. For one reason, this was the first time I'd ever been this close to him. As I said, the old man had always tended to him before. The second reason was, I had a pretty good idea of what was going to happen out there. I was fairly certain that this would be a one-way trip for old Doc.

Because Doc's movements were so labored, it took us quite a while to get out to the tree where the old man was waiting. Doc let out a soft nicker as we approached, almost as if to greet him.

"Bring him right over here," the old man said, quietly, as he stood next to the large hole he had dug in the ground. In his hand was a pistol. It had a very long barrel and looked brand new. It was the type of gun that I'd seen so many times in all the western movies and TV shows, and I couldn't help but stare at it.

"Isn't it something?" the old man asked, with a smile. "It's a Smith and Wessen Schofield, .45-caliber. My father bought it used in 1888 on his eighteenth birthday. He gave it to me just before he died back in '27."

"I've never seen one," I said, as I moved Doc into position next to the pit and then walked to the old man's side. "It looks like new."

"It's always been well cared for," he said, with a hint of sadness in his voice as he walked over and gently stroked Doc on the forehead. Again the horse let out a soft nicker.

After standing quietly in front of the horse for a few seconds, he took a deep breath and stepped directly backwards until he was arm's length from Doc's head.

"Have you ever seen this done before?" he asked, matter-of-factly.

"No," I replied.

Doc let out a soft nicker as we approached, almost as if to greet him.

"Most people who've never done this think that when you shoot the animal, you're supposed to shoot him between the eyes," he said. "That isn't right. If you shoot him there, you'll miss the brain altogether. What you want to do is draw a line from the left ear to the right eye, and from the right ear to the left eye. Where the lines intersect is where you put the bullet."

"Yes sir," I said, as I felt my heart begin to race.

"There'll be some blood," he warned, as he began to raise the pistol. "Mostly out of his nose, but he'll be dead by then."

He pointed the gun at Doc's forehead, hesitated for a second, then pulled the trigger. The noise the gun made was louder than I had expected, and it startled me to the point where I felt myself jump backwards.

Doc dropped immediately, landing only inches from the hole's opening. He was obviously dead before he hit the ground, but still the old man checked for a pulse. As expected, he found none. He turned and walked over to where a brown canvas satchel sat on the ground. He reached inside, pulled out an old-time gun belt, put the pistol back in its holster and returned it to the satchel. He came back over to where Doc was lying, bent down, and grabbed hold of his outstretched front legs.

"If you'll go ahead and grab his back legs," he said, looking up at me, "we'll roll him up on his back. He should just slide into the hole then."

I bent down and took ahold of his legs. On the count of three, we gently rolled Doc onto his back and, as the old man predicted, he slid into the hole.

"You want me to help cover him up?" I asked, looking at the horse.

The old man came over to where I was standing, laid his hand on my shoulder, and said quietly, "No, thanks. I'll do it."

As I turned to head back to the barn, several questions began to pop into my head. The biggest one was why had the old man gone out of his way to bury this crippled-up, skinny, old horse. It wasn't like him. I'd seen a lot of horses pass through the place, possibly hundreds. It was his business, buying and selling. I also knew for a fact that some of those horses had gone straight to slaughter and never once had the old man batted an eye while selling them. Even if horses died on the place, he'd always had the renderer come and pick them up. He never buried them. I couldn't understand it.

Two hours later, the old man came walking up to the barn, a shovel in one hand and his brown canvas satchel in the other.

"Do you mind if I ask you a question?" I asked, as he approached.

"No," he replied. "What do you need to know?"

"I was wondering," I started. "How come you buried old Doc? I mean, I've never seen you do that before."

He set the satchel inside the cab of the old pickup and handed me the shovel. He then lit up a cigarette and said quietly, "Because I owed it to him."

The tone in his voice told me that this was not a subject open for discussion. It was also the last time I would ever bring it up. Still, as if to tell me there were no hard feelings for me sticking my nose in his business, he looked at me with a smile and said, "I'll tell you one thing, though. That dirt sure goes back in the hole a helluva lot easier than it comes out."

"I bet that's true," I replied, with a sheepish grin.

Shortly after that, the old man went out behind the barn to where several pieces of old horse-drawn machinery were. There was an old one-bottom plow, a rake, sickle, potato digger, and several buckboard running gears. There was also an old, dilapidated beet wagon. It was this wagon that he went to and pried off two boards.

The next two days he spent in his workshop fashioning a grave marker out of the boards. He planed one edge of each of the boards and glued them together so that they made one wide board. He then hand-carved his carefully chosen words into the board before placing it at the head of Doc's resting place.

It took me two days to get up the nerve to walk out and read what the old man had put on the marker. Even then, I made sure to do it when he wasn't around so as not to seem as though I was prying again.

I'd been a little puzzled by the old man's reasons for burying the horse to begin with, but the words on the marker puzzled me even more. It read, simply:

DOC HE TAUGHT WELL

Now, I'd heard of horses referred to as "teachers" before. It usually meant that the horse was so well trained that he would actually teach a poor rider how to ride better. It's almost the same as a horse that is referred to as a "babysitter." This means that the horse is so quiet and well trained that he does his best not to allow any harm to come to his rider, no matter how inexperienced the rider is.

I'd seen an awful lot of these "teachers" and "babysitters" pass through the place. The old man, while always treating them well, never once treated them with the reverence that he had Doc. I was sure that whatever it was Doc had taught the old man, or more importantly, what the old man had learned, was the reason the old man had felt so strongly about him. It may have even been the key to the old man's success as a horseman.

My dream, from the very beginning, was someday to become as good with horses as the old man was. To accomplish this dream, I knew that I'd have to work hard. I also knew

It took me two days to get up the nerve.

that I'd have to try to learn what he already knew and then be able to apply it successfully. Unfortunately, the one horse that appeared to have the biggest impact on him was now gone. With Doc went any chance that I may have had to learn from him as the old man had.

Surely, I thought to myself, there must be another horse out there that could do the same thing for me that Doc had done for the old man.

With this thought in mind, my search began for the horse that could show me the secret that the old man had learned. With each horse that I worked with over the next several years, I asked myself the same question—what is this horse trying to teach me? Unfortunately, nothing that I was learning by working with those horses jumped out at me as being the secret I was searching for.

As a result, as time went by, the question slowly went from, "What is this horse trying to teach me?" to, "What can I teach this horse?" In fact, I had gotten so far away from the original question that the incident with Doc and the words on his marker had become nothing more than a seldom-remembered, dusty old memory.

Then I met Little John Beam.

Little John Beam, or John for short, was a retired roping horse. In his time, he'd been very good at what he did, carrying two kids to the national finals in Little Britches Rodeo. In his later years, no longer having the speed that he needed to be competitive, he'd been sold to a dude string. There, his early days of countless hard stops and turns caught up with him. He began to develop ringbone, a calcification of the bone, in both front ankles. He was also starting to show symptoms of being arthritic in both knees, more so in his right. Feeling that the rigors of being in a dude string would further add to his injuries, he was sold again.

He was purchased by a vet student and friend of mine, Dave Schneider. Over the next two years, Dave and John would become great friends and companions. Once in a while, they would even attend jackpot ropings where once again John would shine. Dave, who at the time was an inexperienced roper, would often comment that it was indeed John that had taught him some of the finer points of roping.

Upon his graduation from vet school, Dave was faced with a dilemma. He had accepted a position at the University of Georgia, but due to the fact that the condition in John's front legs had begun to worsen slightly, he feared that taking John along and forcing him into a long trailer ride would do him more harm than good. He decided that it might be best to leave John here in Colorado. Dave asked if I would be willing to watch over and care for John in his absence, and I happily agreed. John was twenty-five years old at the time.

John stayed with me for the next three years, mostly in a state of semi-retirement. Occasionally he would be used to take youngsters on their first horseback ride or for adults who had lost their nerve due to a bad fall.

By the third summer, the arthritis in his right knee had become so bad that the joint was the size of a softball. He had also lost a few teeth over the past winter, which made keeping weight on him a little difficult. It was obvious that he probably would not fare well through another winter, so on a visit to Colorado that summer, Dave examined him and decided that before the heavy weather of the winter set in, he would have John put to sleep.

Still, the summer was a good one for John. Due to his increasing lameness, however, riding him was now out of the question. He continued to be useful, though, by playing the part of babysitter to a young Arab gelding that had recently lost his pasture mate.

John took to his babysitting job with great enthusiasm and seemed to thrive on the lush green pasture. Unfortunately, the young gelding's owner lost the lease on the pasture, and I was forced to move John to the ranch where I was doing some training. We put John in a large run with a shelter so that his feed could be watched carefully, and for a week or so he seemed to get along pretty well. By mid-August, however, I began to see a marked change in him. He appeared to be becoming more and more depressed with each passing day, and he was steadily losing weight even though he always had plenty of feed in front of him. Even turning him out to pasture seemed to have no effect on his disposition.

Thinking that there may be something physically wrong with him, I had the local vet give him the once over.

"Nothing seems to be wrong," the vet commented, after examining him. "He's just showing his age."

The following Wednesday morning, while working a colt in the nearby round pen, I looked over and noticed that John appeared to be in a little better spirits than he had been recently. He was playing across the fence with the horse in the pen next to him, and occasionally he would break into a trot inside the pen, shaking his head and squealing like a colt. By midmorning, however, he began to show signs that perhaps he wasn't in as high spirits as I had originally thought. Looking exhausted, he went over to his water tank and began kicking it with his front foot. He did this non-stop for nearly ten minutes before quitting. He then turned, looked directly at me, and whinnied.

I thought maybe he was trying to tell me that his tank was empty or perhaps too dirty for him to drink out of, so I walked over to check it. I found the tank over half full with clean spring water. As I stood looking at it, John walked over to the gate and let out a low nicker, as if to say, "Hey, let me out of here." Unfortunately, all the turnout areas were being used at the time so I was forced to leave him in his pen.

"Sorry, buddy," I said, petting him on his forehead. "You'll have to wait a little bit."

I went back to the round pen and continued what I was doing. John went back to kicking his water tank. It wasn't until about lunch time that there was finally an open area to turn him out in. But, instead of exercising himself like I thought he would, he simply stood at the gate, kicking it with his front foot and nickering at me. This went on for about an hour before I went and put him back in his pen. As we walked towards the pen, he stopped dead in his tracks three times in obvious protest about going back. Then, once inside, he went right back to kicking the water tank. He also went over and kicked the feed trough, his wooden shelter, the metal side panels, and the gate. While doing all of this, he would also stop periodically, look directly at me, and whinny.

Because of the fuss he was making, I began to become concerned that he might be colicking, but after a quick check of his temperature, gut sounds, and membrane color, I ruled that out.

By 4:30 that afternoon, he had settled back down to kicking the water tank only occasionally. Feeling that there was nothing I could do to make him happy, I climbed in my truck and began to head for home. As I slowly rolled past his pen, he ran up to the fence and let out a loud high-pitched squeal. I stopped the truck, gave him a long hard look to make sure he was okay, then continued on. I had no sooner gotten home and in the door than the phone rang. On the other end of the line was one of the women down at the ranch.

"Sorry to bother you," she said, "but John's down, and we can't get him up."

"Down?" I asked. "Is he colicking?"

"No," she replied. "He's cast himself. We've got his feet out of the fence, but he still doesn't want to get up." I didn't like the sound of that. It wasn't at all like John. He'd been acting up all day and now this. Something was wrong.

"Do you want me to call a vet?" she asked.

"No," I replied. "Just keep trying to get him up. I'll be right there."

By the time I reached the ranch, she and another gal had successfully gotten John to his feet and were standing with him outside his pen. He looked awful. The hairs of his coat were sticking up in all different directions, one hind foot was cocked, his eyes were nearly closed, and his bottom lip was just hanging. He had a look of total and complete resignation about him, a look I hadn't seen since the day the old man put Doc to sleep.

John saw me out of the corner of his eye, slowly turned his head, and let out a low, soft nicker. It was as if he was saying, I'm okay now. He'll know what to do.

I watched him carefully for nearly ten minutes. During that time, he tried to walk off a couple of times. He bumped me with his head almost continuously and nearly collapsed once. It's very hard to explain the feeling I was getting from him, but one thing was for sure, he didn't want to be where he was any longer.

"He looks pretty bad," I heard myself say, after giving the situation careful thought. "I'm going to put him down."

"I don't think we'll be able to get a renderer here till tomorrow," one of the women said. "We can't just leave him here."

"No renderer is going to get this horse," I said bluntly.

"Well, what are you going to do with him?" she asked.

"Don't worry about that," I replied. "I'll find a spot for him. There's a lot of ground around here that nobody ever gets near."

It was true. The ranch covered nearly three thousand acres of foothills. Finding a spot for John to rest wouldn't be a problem. The problem would be finding one that was close enough for John to walk to, but far enough out that he wouldn't be bothered and where he wouldn't bother others.

I went to the truck and pulled out my rifle and a handful of shells. I then took ahold of John's lead rope, and we headed into the hills. We walked for nearly a mile through a narrow gully before finding a small game trail carved into the red clay. The trail zigzagged its way up the side of the steep hill that lay before us.

I was fairly certain that somewhere along that trail would be the perfect spot for John. After resting for a short time at the bottom, we turned and started up. The trail was very narrow and consisted of little more than a countless series of switchbacks that wound their way through patches of mountain mahogany bushes. This made walking on the trail very difficult for both of us, and it was certainly not helped by the fact that the hillside we were on was very steep and treacherous.

As we neared the top of the hill, we came upon a spot where the trail, which had all but disappeared, widened. This was it. There was just enough room for John to lie down and be comfortable, and it was far enough out of the way to where he wouldn't be bothered. It also appeared that he'd gone as far as he was going to go. He looked very tired.

I was pretty sure that it would only be a matter of time before he'd want to lie down. I told myself that I'd wait for him to do that, no matter how long it took, before I put him to sleep. In a sense, I wanted him to pick his own time to leave.

He had been a good horse over the years and had always done what was asked of him. He'd given of himself on countless occasions and now as his life was coming to an end, this was the only thing that I could give back. I didn't care if it took all night. I wouldn't do anything until he was lying down.

I leaned my unloaded gun up against a nearby bush and took a seat next to him on a large rock. He closed his eyes and appeared to go to sleep. As he stood resting, I looked out across the valley that lay below us. The grass was unusually green for that time of year, due mostly to the abundance of rain we'd had that summer. I thought of how nice a view this was and how unfortunate it was that I was seeing it under these circumstances.

After about twenty minutes, John slowly opened his eyes, looked around for a minute, then laboriously laid down. He lay with his legs up underneath himself for a few seconds, then slowly rolled over onto his left side. I knelt down, having to pick his head up off the ground in order to unbuckle and remove his halter. As I made my way over to my gun, I heard him let out a long and restful sigh. Slowly I loaded the rifle with one bullet, took a deep breath, and turned back to where he was lying.

"God, I hate this," I heard myself say, as I knelt down by his head and took aim with the rifle.

As I was about to pull the trigger, I suddenly noticed that John wasn't breathing. I quickly reached down and felt for a pulse from the artery in his neck. There was none. His eye was open and his pupil dilated, and every muscle in his body was relaxed. I couldn't believe it. Just like that, he was gone.

I sat down in the red clay next to his head and lightly stroked his neck.

"So this is what you were trying to tell me all day," I said, quietly. "You didn't want to die in that damned old pen." I suddenly felt very small. Here I'd been all these years trying to find ways to communicate with horses. Finally, one tries to communicate with me, and I nearly blow it.

"Well, by God," I said, getting to my feet after nearly twenty minutes and brushing the red dust from my jeans. "You sure taught me a lesson. You can bet I'll never let something like this get past me again."

I began to make my way back down the same path we'd come up on nearly an hour earlier. The sun was just beginning to set, which made the clay I was walking on seem even redder, and the coolness of the night was just beginning to set in. I'd gotten all the way down to the narrow gully when suddenly, the meaning of the words I'd spoken on the hill hit me.

"You sure taught me a lesson," I had said. That lesson was to pay more attention when horses are trying to communicate with me. I finally understood what had eluded me all those years.

Communication, not us communicating to them, but them communicating to us.

We're always so busy trying to show horses what we want from them that we don't take the time to listen to what they're trying to say back.

Here had been a horse, John, that had tried all day to get me to listen to what he had to say. Finally, when all attempts at that had failed, he did the one thing that he knew would not be ignored. He cast himself. He knew it would just be a matter of time before somebody would come along and spot him with his legs caught in the fence. Certainly they'd get his legs out, get him to his feet, and then get him out of the pen to make sure he was all right, which was exactly what he wanted.

Now, I'm sure that there are folks out there who would say the whole incident was nothing but a series of coincidences. Maybe they're right. But, what if they're wrong? How big a tragedy would it be to have an animal trying literally to talk to us, but we, not having the insight to think that it could actually be happening, ignore him?

The way I see it, just about the only time we ever do any communicating to the horse at all is when we're trying to show him how to respond properly to us. On the other hand, when a horse communicates to us, he's usually trying to show us what he's thinking or feeling. In a sense, he's trying to teach us about himself and how to communicate on his level. We just never take the time to put ourselves in the role of the student and learn from what he's trying to teach.

Suddenly it all made sense. After nearly twenty-five years, I finally understood what the words "He Taught Well" on Doc's marker meant.

As I made my way through the narrow gully, I couldn't help but stop and look back up the hill to where John's resting place was. I wished that the old man had been there so I could have told him that I, too, had seen the teacher. But for me, the teacher wasn't just one horse. It was many horses.

It was a mare snubbed to a post in a round pen years ago. Another that had run through a barbed wire fence, and one that had been severely abused. It was a horse that pulled me down a hill, and one that didn't want to load into a trailer. It was a paint mare that stepped on my hand, a bay gelding that refused to stop, and a sorrel mare that loosened my front tooth.

It was a horse named Doc, one named John, and it was a gray-haired old man with skin like leather who smoked too much. It was a lifetime of daily lessons learned from teachers too numerous to mention, and as I turned to continue on my way with dusk settling in across the valley, I could truly say: they all taught well.

NOTES FOR SEEING THE TEACHER

Over the years I have had the opportunity to go back and visit the place where Walter, "the old man," and I spent so much time together back when I was a kid. Slowly but surely the area has been swallowed up by houses, condominiums, schools, soccer fields, and paved streets. One of the final lots to be developed was where the old man's barns, arena, and round pen once were. Even though everything was growing up around the lot, it had always been easy to see from the road.

A few years back, my wife and I happened to be in the area and decided to go see what, if anything, was left of the lot. As we drove past the spot where the driveway used to be I was saddened to find it, too, was now gone. We drove a little farther on and found a side street that appeared to head back in the general direction of where the barns used to be. Having assumed it had been developed along with the rest of the area, I was interested to see what had been built on the land and as a result, we turned and drove down the street.

Much to our surprise, as we rounded the next corner we found that the lot where the barns once stood were still vacant! It was the only lot in the area not developed and was covered by tall grass and wildflowers. We didn't see any "No Trespassing" signs so we got out of the truck and walked around for a bit. I pointed out to Crissi where the barns and driveway used to be, and where the fence lines and arenas once stood. We walked to the area where the south fence line had been and found the remainder of a nearly forty-year-old wooden post laying in the grass I had once planted nearby as the corner of the fence line.

After a half hour or so, we headed back toward the truck when I suddenly recognized the old cottonwood tree under which Doc, the horse I spoke about in this chapter, had been buried. The tree was now right on the fence line between a large house to the north and the vacant lot we were on and cast its considerable shadow into the backyard of the neighboring house, supplying a cool place for family gatherings and offering relief from the heat of the summer. I pointed out the tree to Crissi and thought about going over and paying my respects to the old horse, but instead we decided to just stand for a few minutes and admire the stately cottonwood from afar.

Both Crissi and I were struck with the fact that while everything around Walter's old horse ranch had been turned into houses and condos, the one place that hadn't been developed was right there where he spent most of his time . . . the place where the barns once stood. There was no trace of the old wooden buildings anymore but in their place trees, grasses, and flowers grew. Things were different there now. Not better or worse. Just different. Not only that, but it was as if that old cottonwood tree was the anchor that still held it all together.

When I look back on this book, I believe I can say the same thing about my work with horses. Things are different now. Not better or worse. Just different. And like that old cottonwood tree, it is the principles about horses, people, and life that I learned from Walter all those years ago that continue to hold it all together.

Horse training, clinics, equine rehabilitation,
and other services provided by Mark Rashid
can be arranged by writing Mark at
P.O. Box 3241, Estes Park, CO 80517.
Comments about his book are also welcome.